LIBERIA

BY DEBRA A. MILLER

LUCENT
BOOKS®

THOMSON
*
GALE

San Diego • Detroit • New York • San Francisco • Cleveland • New Haven, Conn. • Waterville, Maine • London • Munich

For more information, contact
Lucent Books
27500 Drake Rd.
Farmington Hills, MI 48331-3535
Or you can visit our Internet site at http://www.gale.com

LIBRARY OF CONGRESS CATALOGING-IN-PUBLICATION DATA

Miller, Debra A.
      Liberia / by Debra A. Miller.
    p. cm. — (Modern nations of the world)
Includes bibliographical references and index.
      ISBN 1-59018-540-4 (alk. paper)
    1. Liberia—Juvenile literature. [1. Liberia.] I. Title. II. Series.
      DT624.M55 2004
      966.62—dc22

                                   2003021488

Printed in the United States of America

CONTENTS

INTRODUCTION

A BROKEN NATION

Liberia, located on the western coast of Africa, is a country in ruins. Once prosperous, it has been torn apart and almost destroyed by years of civil war. Ever since a military coup in 1980, the country's fortunes have gone downhill as corrupt and hated leaders used Liberian resources for their own benefit and failed to invest in the country's economy or people. The misrule inspired Liberians to form rebel groups that fought government troops and tried to take over the government, plunging the country into a series of civil wars that further devastated the country's economy and infrastructure. The civilian population has been caught in the middle, suffering and dying as they fled from their homes and became refugees in Liberia and neighboring countries. Ironically, the chaos and devastation in Liberia came only after Liberians of tribal descent came to power, overthrowing the century-long dominance of a group of powerful Liberians whose ancestors, American slaves, founded the country in 1847.

These original founders of Liberia, called Americo-Liberians, based the African country on the structure of the United States. Liberia's government is a republic, with a president, a house, and a senate, just like the United States. Its cities and towns, such as its capital of Monrovia, are named after U.S. presidents, and its counties have American names like Virginia, Maryland, and New Georgia. Its government buildings are called Capitol Hill, and the main hospital is called the JFK Medical Center. Much of its culture is borrowed American culture. Even the Liberian flag is similar to the U.S. flag, with red and white stripes and a star in a blue field.

Beginning in World War II, the U.S. government and American companies helped build many improvements in Liberia, including an international airport, railroads, and a modern seaport. With this help, and under the rule of the Americo-Liberians, Liberia prospered in many ways. Beginning in the 1950s and 1960s, its economy grew, its exports increased, and it provided expanded education, jobs, and opportunities for many Liberians, including Liberians from tribal backgrounds.

Liberia's American-descended founders, however, considered themselves superior to indigenous Liberians. They arrogantly held on to power and failed to give the great majority of indigenous Liberians a stake in the government, leading to a 1980 military coup that ended Americo-Liberian rule and began a new era for Liberia. Unfortunately, the new Liberia was marked by unchecked government corruption, a lack of investment in the economy or education, growing poverty and unemployment, and a chain of brutal civil wars that destroyed the country.

A Liberian family files with their belongings through a military checkpoint. Many Liberians lost everything as a result of a series of civil wars.

In 2003, Liberians begged the United States to come to their aid and lead an international peacekeeping force to stabilize and rebuild their country. In August 2003, a fragile peace was established after President Charles Taylor agreed to step down and a West African peacekeeping force, accompanied by a few American troops, arrived in Liberia. The United Nations (UN) took over the peacekeeping operation in October 2003 and began a process of reconstruction and disarmament. Elections are planned for 2005. However, this is but the most recent of many efforts in the last decade to permanently end the fighting in Liberia. The world, and most of all Liberians, pray that this peace mission will work so that Liberia can move forward to a more prosperous and peaceful future.

A Tropical Place

Liberia is a small, tropical country on the west coast of central Africa, just a few degrees north of the equator—a land where it is always summer. Its shoreline faces the Atlantic Ocean to the southwest, and its other borders are shared by three African countries—Sierra Leone to the west, Guinea to the north, and Côte d'Ivoire (Ivory Coast) to the east. Although only about the size of the state of Tennessee, the country boasts three different geographical areas: coastal plains, low plateaus, and high mountains. Liberia's location, climate, and varied geography make it rich in natural resources, the building blocks for a thriving economy and country.

Plains, Hills, and Mountains

Unlike many African nations, Liberia is not landlocked; it occupies 350 miles of the western Africa coastline next to the Atlantic Ocean. The land along the seacoast of Liberia extends about 20 to 30 miles inland and is mostly a straight shoreline, broken by numerous rivers and a few rocky cliffs. For example, the northern-most shoreline features Cape Mount, a mountainous landmark that juts out of the sea to a height of over one thousand feet. Farther south is a similar protrusion, called Cape Mesurado, the site of Liberia's capital city, Monrovia. The remainder of Liberia's coastline is more uniform, interspersed with rivers, whose estuaries often form swampy areas or tidal pools near the beach, surrounded by groves of tropical plants such as mangrove and palms.

This coastal plain is flat, fertile, and blessed with ample rain. For these reasons, it also is the most developed and populated part of Liberia. Although once all of Liberia was covered with tropical rain forests, the coastal plains have largely been denuded of forests and are now filled instead with small farms, larger plantations, grassy open spaces, and areas of second-growth trees or brush. Low-lying areas are often flooded by rain, creating many seasonal or permanent

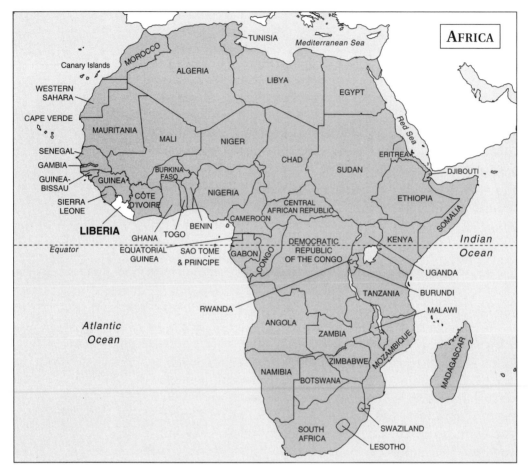

swamps, lagoons, and lakes. Besides the capital city of Monrovia, two other cities, Buchanan and Harbel, are located along or near the northern coast, and two more, Greenville and Harper, are situated along the southern coastline.

Behind the coastal plains are hills, low mountains (with elevations between five hundred and twenty-three hundred feet), and broad valleys. These areas receive abundant rainfall, although less than the coast, and are covered with tropical rain forests. Some of the forest has been cleared, especially in the northeastern part of the country inland from Monrovia, but a good deal of virgin rain forest remains, sparsely inhabited by just a few tribal villages and farms. In fact, as noted in a 1996 Voice of America broadcast, "Liberia is one of the last West African countries with significant rain forests. Semi-deciduous forests still cover nearly one-half of the country."[1]

The deep interior of Liberia is mountainous, marked by three sets of high mountains—the Guinea Highlands in the north near the border with Guinea, the Walo and Wangisi Mountains in the far north, and the Nimba Mountains farther south, on the border where Liberia, Guinea, and Côte d'Ivoire meet. Mountain ranges reach heights of over 4,000 feet. Liberia's highest mountain at 4,528 feet is Mount Wutivi, located in the Nimba mountain range. Mountain areas lack the heavy rainfall and dense forests of the lower elevations; instead, trees and sometimes grassy areas are found primarily in the mountain valleys.

Harper is a small city located on Liberia's southern coast. Liberia's coastal plains are the country's most developed and populated areas.

RIVERS AND LAKES

Liberia's rivers all flow in one direction—from the country's interior mountains and hills southwest toward the sea. Although rainfall varies, causing overflow during rainy seasons and lower levels during drier times, all the rivers run relatively high year round. Despite this fact, none of the rivers are navigable for any great distance because of rapids, sandbars, rocks, and narrow channels. Yet the rivers are valuable for irrigating farmland and for fishing.

The Saint Paul River is probably the most important river in Liberia; it was used by early settlers to gain access to inland areas. It runs for 125 miles, from the Guinea Highlands to its exit to the ocean a few miles north of Monrovia. Unlike

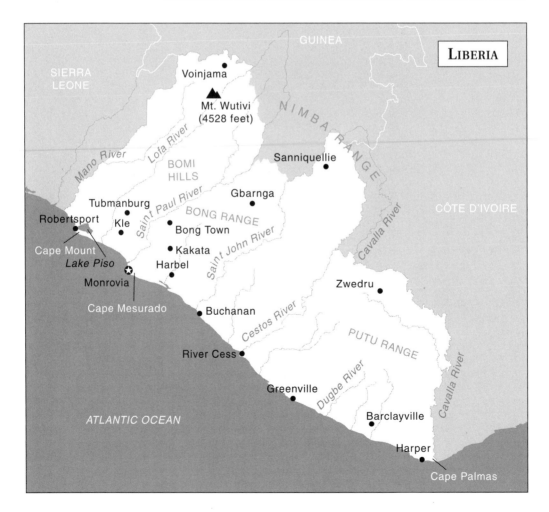

many other rivers in Liberia, it is partially navigable for about 18 miles from Monrovia to its first set of rapids at White Plains. About 35 miles south of the Saint Paul River is the Farmington River, a much shorter stream but one that is also navigable for about 15 miles inland, allowing rubber products to be shipped from the city of Harbel, which is located on the river, to the sea. The northern-most river is the Mano River, which forms part of the border with Sierra Leone. Running about 10 to 20 miles south and parallel to the Mano is the Loffa River, known for its many rapids.

Southern rivers include the Saint John River, which flows from an area northwest of the Nimba Mountains and reaches the sea near the middle of Liberia, and the Cess River, which is located about 150 miles southeast of the Saint John River and flows from the country of Côte d'Ivoire across the southern part of Liberia. Liberia's only other major river is the Cavalla River, which forms much of the country's southeast border with Côte d'Ivoire and is also partially navigable to about 50 miles inland. Between the Cess River and the Cavalla River, a number of small, short streams flow into the ocean.

In addition to its rivers and streams, Liberia contains two notable lakes or lagoons. The first is Lake Piso, located inland from Cape Mount in northern Liberia. It became a tourist area after the construction of a highway linking it to other parts of the country (although Liberia's civil war has kept most tourists away). The second area is Mesurado Lagoon, a body of water behind Cape Mesurado in Monrovia.

Climate

Because Liberia is located almost on the equator, its climate is almost constantly moist and warm, with very little variation in temperature or rainfall. Temperatures range from nighttime lows of about fifty degrees Fahrenheit to daytime highs of about ninety degrees Fahrenheit. Rainfall measures about two hundred inches per year along the coast to seventy inches per year in Liberia's interior. However, as noted by Liberian author Dr. C. Abayomi Cassell, Liberians still refer to two seasons: "The wet season and the dry season, or, in common parlance, 'the rains' and 'the dries,' the former corresponding nearly to summer and autumn, and the latter to winter and spring." [2] This differentiation refers to relatively slight changes in weather.

For example, although some rain falls throughout the year, more precipitation and cooler daytime temperatures (seventy-five to eighty degrees Fahrenheit) are likely between March and October, and less rain and hotter conditions (eighty to ninety degrees Fahrenheit) usually occur between December and March. The rainy season also typically experiences a sharp drop in precipitation for a few weeks in July and August, a period known as the "middle dries."

Liberia's constant heat is offset by reliable ocean breezes, which blow inland for most of the day. At night, especially in December, January, and February, land winds (called harmattan) carry dry air and dust from northeastern Africa's deserts across the country. Sometimes, usually between May and November, land breezes blow southwesterly, creating monsoonal conditions and high humidity in Liberia. The harmattan winds tend to occur in northern Liberia, while monsoonal winds affect the southern part of the country.

Liberia's predominant climate feature, however, is its heavy rainfall, which allows the country to escape the drought that afflicts much of Africa. The country's average rainfall is about 120 to 150 inches, with more rain in coastal areas and less inland. Heavy monsoons along the coast during the wet season account for most of this rainfall; these storms can range from heavy showers that last for a few hours to intense downpours that last several days. Indeed, Liberia's heavy rains can be seen in weather statistics; for example, in July 1955, Monrovia recorded 14.30 inches of rain in twenty-four hours, and in 1960, 13 inches fell in just a few hours.

PLANTS AND WILDLIFE

Liberia's varied geography, warm climate, and abundant rainfall have produced a wide variety of vegetation and wildlife. The country's most prominent asset is its virgin rain forests. These forests consist largely of numerous types of hardwood or broadleaf trees that do not lose their leaves, such as red oak (valuable in construction), whismore (a medium hardwood), and sassywood (whose bark produces a poison). The trees grow as high as two hundred feet, providing a canopy of shade and filtered sunlight conducive to the growth of many plant species; the most striking are spectacular climbing vines hundreds of feet long, such as the calamus palm, and masses of orchids.

LIBERIA'S PYGMY HIPPOPOTAMUS

One of the rare animal species that lives in Liberia's dense rain forests is *Hippopotamus liberiensis*, a pygmy hippopotamus. The hippo grows to a height of about two to three feet, is about four to five feet long, and weighs between 350 and 600 pounds. It has smooth, hairless skin and is a black/brown/purple color, often with pink cheeks. It has a stubby tail of yellow hair. The pygmy hippopotamus was not discovered until the late 1800s, perhaps because it is a solitary and primarily nocturnal animal. The hippos live in the thick underbrush of tropical forests, near rivers or streams. They rest or sleep most of the morning and afternoon, and come out to feed in the late afternoon. They are most active at night. The pygmy hippos eat fallen fruits, aquatic plants, grass, and leaves of tropical plants. While foraging, they make tunnels deep into the dense brush of the rain forests. African natives hunt pygmy hippos for their meat. As a species, the pygmy hippo is listed as vulnerable.

A pygmy hippopotamus calf looks for food. African natives hunt pygmy hippos as food.

The rain forests also support a wide range of animal life, including 568 species of birds, 9 of which are endangered, and several rare animal species, including the pygmy hippopotamus, the white-breasted guinea fowl, Jentink's duiker (a very rare deerlike creature), the Diana monkey, and the Liberian mongoose. Other animals can also be found in Liberia, such as crocodiles, snakes (including the python and

The Threat to Liberia's Rain Forests

Liberia's rain forests are threatened by a dramatic increase in timber cutting that began during the administration of ex-president Charles Taylor. What was once a virtually untouched virgin jungle that covered almost half of the country is now crisscrossed by strips of deforested bush and roads. The threat comes from multinational companies that seek to cut down the trees in Liberia, many of which are valuable African hardwoods. In 1999, for example, the government of Liberia granted timber concessions to a company from Indonesia, the Oriental Timber Company (OTC), in an area of southeastern Liberia covering as much as 2.5 million acres. The company began cutting trees down so quickly that some predicted that Liberia's rain forests could disappear in as little as ten years.

Timber is one of the only Liberian industries remaining after years of civil war, and it became a major source of revenue for the government headed by Taylor. In 1999, Taylor assumed complete control over the export of Liberia's natural resources, including its forests, and he used these timber resources to pay for the war. He also has been accused of stealing funds from Liberia for his own personal use. In 2001, the United Nations (UN) banned Liberia's trading of diamonds, because Taylor was using the profits to support rebels fighting in the neighboring country of Sierra Leone. In May 2002, the UN extended the earlier ban on diamonds for a year and added a ten-month ban on Liberian timber. Now that Taylor has resigned as president and left Liberia, environmentalists hope that Liberia's next leaders will better manage and protect its rain forest treasure.

The timber trade is one of Liberia's main sources of revenue, but the industry has destroyed much of the country's rain forest.

cobras), chimpanzees, monkeys, the bongo antelope, and leopards. Elephants, water buffalo, and other large animal species once were abundant, but now are very scarce because of hunting.

In addition to the rain forest and its bounty, Liberia has other plant and animal assets. Rubber trees, which grow as high as two hundred feet and produce latex, are used to make commercial rubber for tires and other products. Other native plants include several varieties of coffee trees, and the kola tree, whose nuts are used in medicines and beverages. Deciduous forests also are abundant in Liberia, producing valuable timber, including a variety of beautiful mahogany wood, cabinet hardwoods, and softwoods. Near the coast, vegetation typically includes dense thickets of mangrove trees in the tidal estuaries, as well as various species of palms, low bushes, grasses, and ferns.

Fish, such as catfish, perch, carp, and a large fish similar to salmon called the hydrocyon, can sometimes be caught in the country's freshwater streams and rivers, but overfishing has largely depleted this resource. Saltwater fish, such as mackerel, mullet, barracuda, snappers, and sharks, are found in Liberia's coastal waters and estuaries. Numerous insects thrive in the tropical climate and many water sites, and can spread diseases such as malaria and sleeping sickness. Mosquitoes, tsetse flies, scorpions, centipedes, termites, and ants seem to be everywhere.

NATURAL RESOURCES

In addition to its rain and climate, Liberia's rich soil makes it an ideal site for a variety of plant life. Aside from the rain forests, this soil produces various agricultural products and tree crops, including the rubber tree, which developed into a highly successful industry that provided many jobs, at least until the recent years of civil war. As of 2001, rubber remained one of Liberia's top agricultural exports; other agricultural products included coffee, cocoa, rice, cassava (tapioca), palm oil, sugarcane, and bananas.

Liberia's soils also account for a large timber and logging industry. Indeed, as American University author Thomas D. Roberts estimated in 1972, "about nine million acres, or over one-third of the land area of the country, is covered by high forest, which with good management could yield at least 2

VISITING LIBERIA

The civil war in Liberia has made traveling to Liberia very dangerous and has disrupted its tourist industry. However, before the war, Liberia was beginning to develop tourism as a source of economic and social development. Indeed, its unique history as a country founded by American slaves, its ethnic diversity, its exotic wildlife, and its tropical beauty make Liberia an interesting and attractive tourist destination. The best time to visit the country is during the dry season, between November and the end of April, when the climate is mostly sunny with gentle breezes. At this time of year, people flock to the beaches, and there is an abundance of entertainment, including live bands and beach parties. In and near Monrovia, there are historic sites such as the Kendeja Culture Center, the Malima Gorblah Village, and the Besao Village, where visitors can see examples of Liberia's indigenous culture and crafts. Monvoria also contains many architectural sites, including old churches and government buildings. Providence Island, the site where the first American settlers landed, is another national historical site of interest to tourists. In addition, Liberia's tourist attractions include its many islands, lakes, and waterfalls. One cautionary note, however, is that visitors may contact diseases such as cholera, hepatitis A, typhoid fever, and malaria while traveling in Liberia.

billion board feet of timber per year indefinitely."[3] This high forest comprises over 225 varieties of deciduous hardwood trees; at least 60 of these varieties are believed to exist in marketable quantities. By 2002, logging had grown to provide 60 percent of Liberia's export revenues. The industry was shut down, however, by the fighting during the country's civil war and by a 2003 UN ban on timber exports from Liberia, the revenues from which the government was using to buy arms.

In addition, Liberia is rich in mineral resources, particularly iron ore, which is present in immense quantities at various sites throughout the country. This wealth was developed after World War II, and with foreign investment, Liberia became one of the world's largest iron ore exporters. The iron ore exploitation also created a construction boom in the country, in which roads, railroads, and harbor facilities were built to handle and ship the mineral deposits. Prior to Liberia's civil war, iron ore production constituted about 20 percent of Liberia's gross domestic product, an indicator of a country's total economic production. The war, however, scared off foreign investors and caused many of the mines to close.

Diamonds are Liberia's second most important mineral export, although they form only a small part of the country's total exports. Mining for this product has continued throughout the war, and many believe the government traded diamonds to acquire arms. Gold has also been found along Liberia's streams, although production was never large and has slowed over the years. Other mineral deposits, such as manganese, platinum, mica, pyrite, graphite, and others, have been indicated in field studies. All minerals in Liberia are the property of the government, and licenses or concessions must be granted by the government in order for private or foreign companies or individuals to mine or prospect, even on private land.

Unlike its soil and mineral resources, Liberia's energy resources are limited. It has no coal or oil deposits, and its only source of power is a hydroelectric potential of about one hundred kilowatts from its many rivers and water rapids. The government built and operated hydroelectric power plants in Monrovia and other areas, and private plants were built in the cities of Harbel and Mount Coffee. The war, however, has largely destroyed the country's electrical grid. As of the late 1990s, only a small amount of electricity was being generated by the government, and by 2003, even the capital of Monrovia was without electric power.

TRANSPORTATION AND COMMUNICATIONS

The poorly developed state of Liberia's transportation system is one of the county's most serious problems, and its condition has only deteriorated during the fourteen years of civil war. Liberia's main interior transportation system once was railroads, which were largely built by mining companies to transport ore from mines in the interior of the country to ports for shipment to buyers. Three rail systems were built— one connecting a mining site at Bomi Hills with the port of Monrovia, a second line connecting mines at Mount Nimba with the port of Buchanan, and a third connecting mines at Bong Hills with Monrovia. The railways, however, were never developed for passenger service. In addition, the line from Mount Nimba was closed after ore production ended in 1989, and the other two lines were shut down by the civil war, when many of the railroad tracks were ripped up and sold for scrap.

As for air travel, Liberia has two major airports—the Roberts International Airport, which was built by the United States near Monrovia during World War II and later improved, and Spriggs Payne Airfield, a smaller airport also near Monrovia. The Roberts site is able to accommodate jet aircraft, and international arrivals and departures operate from there. Spriggs primarily services smaller aircraft. A number of much smaller airstrips also exist throughout the country and are used by small single- and twin-engine planes.

Although in 1964 there were more than twelve hundred miles of publicly constructed roads, Liberia today has few paved roads. After the roads were built, their maintenance was neglected, and rains and flooding slowly eroded them. In addition, many of the roads and bridges have been damaged or destroyed during the country's long civil war. Those roadways that do exist for public travel are in bad shape and primarily connect the capital city of Monrovia with other parts of the country and with neighboring countries.

Finally, although it is located on the Atlantic Ocean, Liberia has no natural, protected ports. As a result, all its harbors are man-made. The main harbor is at Bushrod Island next to Monrovia; it was constructed with U.S. and mining companies' help by creating two rock breakwaters and is large enough to accommodate iron ore shipping vessels and medium-sized cargo ships. In order to encourage industry, the Monrovia port is operated as a free port, which means that merchandise may be stored, processed, repackaged, or used in manufacturing without the payment of duty, or taxes. Other ports were built by mining and rubber companies at the cities of Buchanan, Greenville, and Harper.

Liberia's communications industry is also still developing. Liberia was one of the first African countries to acquire telephone and radio communications, and in the 1960s it invested $7 million to expand and modernize its telecommunications industry. According to the U.S. Central Intelligence Agency, Liberia in 2000 had about 6,700 telephone lines operating through a microwave radio relay network in Monrovia. In addition, the country had seven FM radio stations and one television station. Estimates projected that there were about 790,000 radios in use in the country, and about 70,000 TVs.

There were two Internet providers, serving approximately five hundred subscribers, and no mobile telephone capability. The war, however, has destroyed most of the communications infrastructure.

An aerial view of Liberia's capital city Monrovia shows two bridges spanning the lagoon. Monrovia is the country's only true urban area.

POPULATION AND CITIES

Liberia's population is centered along the coast, particularly the northern coastal area near the capital of Monrovia; the interior of the country is not heavily populated, except for small tribal villages. The country's total population as of July 2003 was estimated at 3,317,176. Most of the population is young by Western standards; the life expectancy in Liberia is only 48.15 years.

The center of Liberia's government, business, transportation, communications, shipping, and social activities is its capital of Monrovia. It was settled in 1822 and today remains the country's largest city and its only truly urban area. As of the late 1990s, Monrovia was home to almost a million people, almost a third of the population. Its name comes from U.S. president James Monroe, who supported the movement in America for relocation of freed slaves back to Africa.

Monrovia is located on Cape Mesurado in northern Liberia at the end of a peninsula, and it is separated from the mainland by a lagoon formed by the Saint Paul River. It is the site of the largest port, the Free Port of Monrovia, and the country's only international airport. It boasts some beautiful areas, such as an impressive capitol building, older residential and diplomatic areas, and the University of Liberia. However, because the population rapidly increased during recent decades, it also contains a number of slums. During the civil war, the city was pounded by mortars and shells and invaded by tens of thousands of refugees seeking shelter and protection from the war. This led to shortages of food, water, and medical supplies, and raised concerns about malnutrition, disease, looting, and crime. Like much of the rest of Liberia, Monrovia will need time to rebound from the war's damage.

A few smaller cities in Liberia include Buchanan, Harbel, and Harper, all built along or near the coast. Buchanan (population: 27,300), located at the mouth of the Saint John River toward the middle of the country's coast, became an important port and shipping point for iron ore brought from the Nimba Mountains. Harbel (population: 17,000) was founded by Firestone and became the rubber production and shipping capital of the country. Harper (population: 20,000), in southern Liberia, was also built by Firestone as a shipping center for the Firestone Cavalla rubber plantation, which was located nearby. Since the war, however, all of Liberia has declined dramatically in prosperity and economic activity.

LAND OF THE FREE

Liberia, whose name means "land of the free," is unique among African nations—it was founded in 1847 by freed American slaves. Unlike many other African nations, therefore, Liberia never existed as a colony of a larger country. Unfortunately, the black American settlers themselves acted like colonizers, ruling over the people from local Liberian tribes and creating ethnic friction and a wide gulf between rich and poor. With U.S. and foreign help, Liberia stabilized and modernized for many decades after World War II under the administration of President William V.S. Tubman and his successor. This stability, however, was destroyed when recession and tribal tensions erupted in the late 1900s, setting Liberia on a downward path toward violence and economic destruction.

THE AFRICAN SLAVE TRADE

Africa's native population comprised small groups or tribes who lived relatively peaceful, sheltered lives as fishermen and farmers. The tribal people of West Africa first made contact with white Europeans when Portuguese traders traveled to the area in the fifteenth century searching for new trade markets and alternate routes to Asia. At first, items traded included ivory and malegueta pepper, but later, slaves became the most important product traded. The Portuguese kidnapped Africans and sent them back to Portugal, Spain, and other European countries to work as unpaid household servants, farmhands, and industrial workers. From the fifteenth to the nineteenth centuries, the slave trade became a booming business for many prominent European nations. Portugal, Spain, France, England, Germany, Denmark, Sweden, the Netherlands, and Belgium all participated in the trading of slaves.

Slaves were obtained in raids on tribal villages, in which men, women, and even children were captured and imprisoned, and then shipped aboard slave ships under brutal conditions to be sold as property. Dr. C. Abayomi Cassell, a

Liberian attorney and writer, describes the horrible inhumanity with which slaves were treated on slave ships:

> When brought aboard ship, the slaves were packed row upon row in the holds, bound together by chains. After a few days, air in the holds became polluted, since natural functions had to be done where they sat. Some of the slaves took sick, others were already sick, disease spread, sometimes like wildfire. Leg, hand or neck irons inflicted wounds which developed infections, and lack of medical attention caused many to die. Many . . . simply died of shame, sorrow and hopelessness. [4]

When the ships reached their destinations, slaves were exhibited at slave markets, usually nude, and interested purchasers examined, weighed, and measured them as though they were animals. Once purchased, they were most often treated like property, forced to work at menial tasks, and treated very badly.

Notably, most of the slaves captured for the slave trade came from interior areas of Africa such as the Congo and the Niger Delta, not from coastal areas such as Liberia. However, tribes living on the coast of what is now Liberia participated in the slave trade by selling slaves captured inland by inland

European slave traders inspect slaves at a West African market. The native tribes of Liberia sold slaves captured inland to such traders.

tribes to European slave traders. Indeed, the coastal tribes became very dependent on the slave trade and fought wars with
other tribes to protect their claim on this commodity.

After the American continents were discovered and settled, the demand for slaves increased. Negroes (as blacks
were called in the nineteenth century) from West Africa were
shipped first to areas colonized by the Portuguese and Span-
ish, such as Brazil, the Dominican Republic, Haiti, Cuba, Ja-
maica, and Puerto Rico. Slavery was first introduced into the
American colonies in 1620, when a Dutch ship transported
twenty West Africans to the Jamestown colony in Virginia.
Thereafter, a total of 3,835,456 slaves were imported into the
United States by England during the colonial period.

THE RESETTLEMENT OF SLAVES IN LIBERIA

By the end of the eighteenth century, many in the United
States and Europe began to question the morality of slavery.
Even Thomas Jefferson, a slave owner himself, argued
against slavery, writing in 1781 that it was a "great political
and moral evil."[5] Jefferson and others proposed emancipa-
tion of slaves. To solve the problem of what to do with slaves
after they were freed, Jefferson and others proposed that they
should be transported to a colony in Africa, the continent
from which they were captured. Support for this resettlement idea grew over the years, as increasing numbers of free
blacks became a concern to many white Americans, who did
not want a multiracial society. In addition, southern slave-
holders determined to keep using slaves feared that too
many freed blacks might threaten their slave practices.

In 1816, these concerns led to the formation of the American Colonization Society (ACS), whose purpose was to resettle free persons of color in Africa. By this time, the number of
freed blacks in the United States had grown to almost a quar-
ter of a million. In 1818, the group sent two representatives to
West Africa to search for an appropriate location for a settlement. They explored areas near Sierra Leone, where Britain
maintained a colony. By 1820, the Colonization Society, with
the support of U.S. president James Monroe, convinced the
U.S. Congress to fund its resettlement project. In 1820, a group
of eighty-eight black settlers—men, women, and children—
and three white agents sailed for Africa on a chartered ship
called the *Elizabeth*.

This first group of settlers landed south of Sierra Leone on Sherba Island, where all three whites and twenty-two of the black settlers died of fever. The remaining settlers moved to Sierra Leone. The following year, in 1821, another group of settlers made the trek to Africa, picked up the survivors of the first group from Sierra Leone, and established the first official settlement on Cape Mesurado, now part of the capital city of Monrovia in modern Liberia. This settlement effort, like the first, fared badly, as tropical diseases and attacks from native tribes killed many.

In 1822, however, things began to improve after the arrival of Jehudi Ashmun, a white Methodist minister and teacher who would become known as the founder of Liberia. Ashmun, as an agent of the ACS, became director of the settlement, and he organized the settlers to build fortifications, form defense teams, clear the land, and begin trade with America. In 1824, the settlement was named Monrovia after U.S. president James Monroe and the colony was called Liberia. The colony was liberally funded by the U.S. Congress, and Ashmun used these monies to buy land and expand the territory of the colony. He built schools, encouraged the establishment of agriculture, sought to root out the vestiges of slave trade along Liberia's coast, and was instrumental in every part of the colony's growth and survival. As Cassell explains, "More than any other single person, [Jehudi Ashmun] molded the shape and destiny of Liberia."[6] By 1828, the date of Ashmun's death, Liberia was home to more than twelve hundred colonists.

THE REPUBLIC OF LIBERIA

As the colony in Liberia prospered, its success ied to the creation of other colonization societies and to additional new settlements in Liberia. Indeed, the 1830s witnessed significant growth and development, and settlements soon stretched all along the Liberian coast while farms spread inland along the rivers. By the late 1830s, there were 2,247 colonists living in Liberia, twenty churches, ten schools, and four printing presses.

Although there was some rivalry, these settlements ultimately found it necessary to cooperate for survival. In 1838, all of the colonies except the colony called Maryland joined together to create the Commonwealth of Liberia and adopt a constitution. Under this new constitution, a governor and

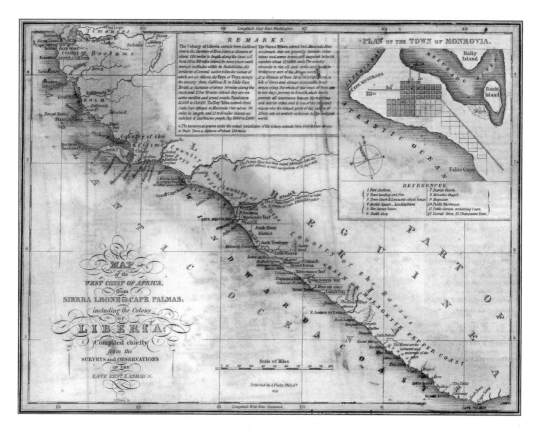

vice governor were appointed by the Colonization Society, a council of Liberians was elected by the colonists, and a supreme court was created. Citizenship was limited to persons of color, and all males over age twenty-one were given the right to vote. However, the Colonization Society retained the right to veto legislation. Thomas Buchanan, brother of U.S. president James Buchanan, was appointed the first governor of Liberia. Buchanan did much to improve Liberia, and after his death, a city in Liberia was named after him.

By 1841, however, the new commonwealth had its first black governor—Joseph Jenkins Roberts, an emigrant to Liberia who was born of mixed blood in Virginia and highly educated. Roberts contributed to the development of Liberia by consolidating all the land along the coast as part of the commonwealth, thwarting efforts by the French to obtain a stake in the area. As a result, by 1845, Liberia was able to claim ownership over the entire coast, from Cape Mount to the Cess River.

Methodist minister Jehudi Ashmun made a number of surveys of Liberia's topography that were incorporated into maps like this one from 1830.

JOSEPH JENKINS ROBERTS, LIBERIA'S FIRST PRESIDENT

Joseph Jenkins Roberts, born in 1809 in Petersburg, Virginia, was Liberia's first president. Roberts was the son of free blacks and was light-skinned, with both white and black ancestors. Roberts first came to Liberia at the age of twenty with his mother and younger brothers. At that time, Liberia had not yet declared its independence and was still a colony. Roberts became a merchant and an unofficial aide to the white governor of the colony, Thomas Buchanan. When Buchanan died in 1842, Roberts was appointed as the first black governor of the colony. As governor, Roberts expanded the colony's territory through

treaties and purchases from tribal chiefs, and made efforts to stop slave trading in Liberia. Roberts helped lead the colony toward independence, and when it became the Republic of Liberia in 1847, he was elected as its first president. Afterward, Roberts sought and acquired recognition of the new country from European countries. When he lost the 1855 election, Roberts helped found and served as the first president of Liberia College, and from 1872 to 1876, he again became president of Liberia.

The son of freed slaves, Joseph Jenkins Roberts became Liberia's first president in 1847.

In addition, Roberts tried to enforce the laws of the commonwealth, particularly in the area of collection of customs duties, or taxes. British traders, however, resisted payment of these duties and complained to the British governor of neighboring Sierra Leone. The governor, in turn, notified Liberia that it would not recognize the right of the Commonwealth of Liberia, essentially a private group, to levy taxes against Britain. After several incidents in which Sierra Leone threatened to seize Liberian territory if the collection of taxes was not stopped, Liberia's Governor Roberts decided that it was necessary for Liberia to break ties with the ACS and become an independent state.

As a result of the British threats, the ACS in January 1846 resolved that "the time had arrived when it was expedient for the people of the Commonwealth of Liberia to take into their own hands the whole work of self-government, including the management of all their foreign relations."[7] In 1846, the commonwealth's legislature met to discuss the idea of independence and begin the process of writing a constitution. In June 1847, a constitutional convention was opened, and on July 26, 1847, with guns booming in the background, Liberia officially proclaimed its independence.

Liberia's Declaration of Independence and constitution were modeled after those of the United States. The new government, like the U.S. system, was a republic with three separate branches (legislative, executive, and judicial). The constitution also provided that "none but Negroes or persons of color shall be admitted to citizenship in this Republic."[8] The territory of the new country included all the land along the coast (and about forty miles inland) from Cape Mount to the Cess River, and ultimately the colony of Maryland south of the Cess River as well. Roberts became the new country's first president.

THE EARLY YEARS

During its first decade as an independent country, Liberia continued to grow. Following his inauguration, President Roberts was successful in getting Great Britain, France, and later the United States to recognize the new country. Also, with the help of American and British naval forces, Roberts crushed the last of the slaver operations on the Liberian coast. In addition, before he left office in 1855, Roberts built schools (including the first college, called Liberia College) and began the process of acquiring more land for the republic; space was needed to accommodate the stream of new emigrants who fled to Liberia before the U.S. Civil War of the 1860s. Roberts retired from politics, but was recognized for his wisdom and contributions; as one contemporary said, "The history of nations is written in the lives of individuals. President Roberts has shaped the destiny of his country, and as much as any other living man has contributed to the moral and physical good of the human race."[9] Despite these early achievements, however, the first phase of Liberia's existence would prove to be a difficult one.

One of the challenges that the country faced, for example, was a series of border disputes with Britain and France. In 1860, a British trader who had developed a successful trading business between Cape Mount and the Sewa River to the northwest claimed that this land did not belong to Liberia, even though Liberia had bought it from native tribes the decade before. Sierra Leone supported the trader's claim, and Britain refused to back Liberia's entitlement to the property, leading Sierra Leone to establish a protectorate over the area. The matter was resolved in 1885 by a treaty that forced Liberia to give up the territory to Sierra Leone in exchange for compensation. In addition, France sought to expand its landholdings in Africa and claimed some of Liberia's territory in southern Liberia southeast of Cape Palmas. When Britain and the United States failed to support Liberia, it was again forced in an 1892 treaty to give up land on its southern border to the French colony of Côte d'Ivoire.

Another difficulty that faced Liberia early in its independence was the strained relationship between the settler population and native tribal people. Certain tribes, such as the Kru and the Grebo, had developed a thriving business trading slaves from the interior of Africa to European slaver ships along Liberia's coastline. The governing settler class, formed from slaves and descendants of slaves, sought to stop this practice. In response, the tribes launched a series of attacks on Liberian settlements, causing trouble for the government of Liberia, which lacked the military forces to completely halt the attacks.

In addition, a culture developed in which the governing settler class, comprising blacks who emigrated from the United States (called Americo-Liberians), considered themselves superior to the native tribal blacks. This attitude resulted in bad treatment of tribal people, who were called aborigines, by the Liberian government. As Liberia extended its influence inland through trade and treaties into the interior forests where many tribes lived (an area referred to by Liberians as the Hinterland), the government began to place greater and greater limits on the power of local tribal chiefs, creating more friction.

THE FIRESTONE LOAN

Yet another problem that the new Liberian republic faced during the late 1800s and early 1900s was its struggling economy. Although Liberians had flourished earlier by trading

agricultural products such as cane sugar, coffee, and other items, foreign competition began to erode this trade base. This economic downturn forced Liberia to turn to high-interest foreign loans as a source of funds, leading the country into an even worse economic and financial crisis.

Liberia appealed to the United States for help, and U.S. president Taft responded in 1909 by appointing a commission to investigate the country's financial affairs. The commission proposed that the United States take full control of Liberia's finances, but this idea was rejected. Instead, an international receivership was created, involving not only America but also France, Germany, and Britain. This enabled Liberia to obtain yet another loan, which only continued the country's financial problems.

By 1926, Liberia became so desperate that, in exchange for a relatively small loan, it permitted an American company, Firestone Tire and Rubber Company, to establish a large commercial rubber plantation in the country. Firestone was looking for a less expensive source of rubber at the time, and Liberia believed that granting a concession to a foreign firm might stimulate its economy. As a result, two agreements

President Roberts lived and worked in this colonial-style mansion in Monrovia. During his presidency, Liberia firmly established itself as an independent nation.

were signed—one giving Firestone a ninety-nine-year lease on 1 million acres of land at six cents (and later eight cents) per acre, and a second extending to Liberia a $5 million loan for a forty-year period to allow it to pay off all its various foreign loans. The proceeds from the loan were to be used to pay off bonds and outstanding foreign debts and to fund construction projects that would benefit both Liberia and Firestone.

The Firestone agreements ultimately enabled Liberia to stabilize financially and improve its infrastructure. In addition to revenues that paid off other debts, Liberia obtained employment for some Liberian citizens, as well as roads, a rail line, port facilities, and telephone and telegraph services—all used by Firestone to transport and ship its rubber products. Unfortunately, these gains came at a heavy cost. Under the terms of the agreements, much of the employment for Liberians was to be in the form of "contract labor" provided by Liberia to Firestone; this essentially meant forced labor by native tribesmen. Also, in exchange for the loan, Liberia agreed to give up control over its financial decisions and to defer to an American financial adviser. As a result, Liberia remained heavily in debt and was unable to progress economically for many years. As economist J.H. Mower has described,

THE FIRESTONE PROJECT TODAY

In 1926, the Firestone Tire and Rubber Company established the first rubber plantation in Harbel, Liberia. Firestone chose Liberia because conditions there are ideal for growing rubber trees. Today, Firestone still occupies a thirty-five thousand-acre facility in Harbel that it calls the "World's Largest Rubber Plantation." It employs fifty-six hundred workers at the plantation. In addition, workers are supposed to receive free housing. However, many of the company houses have been destroyed during Liberia's civil war, and many workers are forced to live in partially destroyed houses or cardboard-and-metal shanties, none of which have water or electricity. In addition, labor activists claim that workers earn only $2.53 a day, and work eight hours a day, six days a week. They also say that Firestone cut its workforce in half in the last decade, increasing the workload for its remaining workers. In addition, the workers say that Difolatan, a chemical that enhances latex production but may cause cancer, is used by Firestone. The company disputes these claims, arguing that its workers earn $5 per day, wages comparable to rubber workers in Thailand or Brazil, and that it no longer uses Difolatan. However, the wage for American workers in Firestone plants is about $19 per hour.

The Firestone Enterprise in Liberia had the elements of the worst of economic exploitation; a large capital investment by a corporation of a powerful nation assuming a dominant position in a weak and backward nation; ... the benefits of the loan going to aid only a minute percentage of the smaller nation's population and [producing] only a slight amount of economic progress. [10]

Decades later, Liberia's economic condition remained poor.

THE TUBMAN PERIOD AND ECONOMIC EXPANSION

World War II finally provided Liberia an opportunity to improve its economic position. Liberia was neutral in the war until 1942, when the United States proposed to build an air base in the small country in return for defending Liberia. Hoping to be on the winning side, Liberia entered the war with the Allies, and allowed the construction of a major airport, military base, and communication and other facilities at Robertsfield, Liberia—today the site of Liberia's only international airport. This U.S. investment was the beginning of an era of economic expansion for the country.

Liberia's better times also were the result of the election, in January 1944, of a new president—President William V.S. Tubman—a member of the True Whig Party, a dominant political party that was made up of educated blacks who wanted to keep European influence out of Liberia and develop the country as a modern nation. Tubman quickly instituted new social and economic policies. For example, Tubman developed the Open Door Policy, which sought to encourage foreign investment in the Liberian economy. As a result of this leadership, and with the help of U.S. and other foreign investment in areas such as mining and agriculture, the Liberian economy rebounded and experienced rapid growth during the 1950s. Jobs were created and schools opened, providing education and opportunities for the first time to many indigenous Liberians. The financial improvements even allowed Liberia to pay off the Firestone loan in 1952.

Tubman also sought to improve relations with native tribes. Tubman announced a National Unification and Integration Policy aimed at unifying all parts of the country and reducing friction between Americo-Liberians and tribal peoples. Shortly after his election, he included members from aboriginal tribes in the national legislature, for the first time providing them some measure of representation in Liberia's government. Later, the interior parts of Liberia were formed into four new counties, providing equal rights and privileges of citizenship to their tribal inhabitants. Tubman also reformed policies that previously had given privileged Liberians special treatment; for example, he eliminated the use of taxpayer funds to pay for the overseas education of children of the elite classes.

PRESIDENT TOLBERT, TUBMAN'S SUCCESSOR

Despite his many good deeds, however, President Tubman's rule had its flaws. He and his followers, for example, ignored the constitution's requirement for a multiparty political system and used state security and force to stay in power. Opposition parties were banned, and citizens often were required to contribute financially to Tubman's True Whig Party, even though it was the only party in existence. Largely as a result of these tactics, Tubman and his party dominated Liberian politics for an extremely long period—from 1944 until 1971.

Tubman's hold on politics, however, reduced the chances of the African tribal majority achieving any real power in Liberia, unless they abandoned ties to their communities and became part of Tubman's Americo-Liberian power elite. Indeed, although Tubman claimed to encourage better treatment of tribespeople, in reality this population, which formed a majority in Liberia, continued to be discriminated against in employment and other areas, and suffered at the hands of the elite classes. For example, during the Tubman era, elite Americo-Liberians were permitted to purchase large tracts of interior lands, displacing many aborigines. Liberia's tribes also remained in poverty. In 1978, approximately 2.5 percent of the Liberian population controlled 70 percent of the country's income, continuing the enormous gap between rich elites and the poor tribal masses. Indeed, most of the benefits of Liberia's growth went to the political elite—members of Tubman's True Whig Party and Americo-Liberians—rather than to poor, indigenous Liberians.

Following his death in 1971, Tubman was succeeded by his vice president, William Richard Tolbert. Tolbert built on Tubman's policies, promising to bring more indigenous Liberians into the government, encourage greater speech and press freedoms, and eliminate government corruption. However,

PRESIDENT WILLIAM V.S. TUBMAN

William Vacanarat Shadrach Tubman was Liberia's president for almost three decades, from 1944 until his death on July 23, 1971, a term longer than any other Liberian president. He was born in Harper, Liberia, in 1895 and was the grandson of slaves set free by Richard Tubman in 1836 in Augusta, Georgia. Tubman thus was part of the Americo-Liberian elite that dominated Liberian politics through the True Whig Party. Nevertheless, President Tubman ruled Liberia during an important time in its history, when it emerged from isolation and began to court foreign investment to develop its economy. Tubman strongly advocated policies to attract this foreign investment, and his efforts made Liberia an economic success during the second half of the twentieth century. By the time he died, Liberia had the largest fleet of trading ships in the world, had the world's largest rubber plantation, and was one of the world's foremost exporters of iron ore. Tubman's policies helped to employ and educate increasing numbers of indigenous Liberians. This eventually led to a political movement of indigenous people who later

rebelled and overthrew the government; this change in government leadership soon destroyed Tubman's economic achievements.

William Tubman served as Liberia's president for nearly three decades.

Tolbert failed to achieve many of his stated goals, and his government became highly corrupt, as evidenced by many reports of dishonest and greedy actions by upper-class, Americo-Liberian government officials. As a result, during Tolbert's presidency, indigenous people became more aware of the inequities in Liberian society and began agitating for multiparty democracy and greater political reforms. Groups, such as the Movement for Justice in Africa (MOJA) and the Progressive Alliance of Liberia (PAL), formed and began spreading their views within the slums of Monrovia and other towns, seeking to build a grassroots movement for political change.

LIBERIA AT WAR

Contemporary Liberia has been characterized by corrupt leadership, civil wars, and the destruction of Liberian peace and prosperity. The long period of stability of the Tubman-Tolbert era ended in 1980, when a military coup brought a brutal military government led by Samuel K. Doe to power. In 1989, an uprising began against the Doe government and resulted in President Doe's murder and the beginning of fourteen years of civil war. Rebel leader Charles Taylor eventually became president, but his rule brought only more corruption, terror, and war for the people of Liberia.

THE 1980 MILITARY COUP

The 1970s provided the fuel for an uprising against Tolbert's government—a worldwide recession that grew out of an oil embargo imposed by oil-producing Arab countries in 1973. Liberia was hit very hard by the recession, as the prices for its trade products fell, providing less revenue for the country, and the prices of imports increased. In 1979, the Liberian government announced a dramatic increase in the price of rice, the staple food of Liberians. The price increase angered the Liberian masses and raised the specter of government corruption; rice was considered essential, and much of the rice that Liberians consumed was either imported or produced by powerful government officials. Indeed, as African military instructor and writer Major Innocent Azubike Nass explains, "It was well known that the president and one of his brothers . . . were connected with the production, importation and sale of rice. In fact, the president himself was known to be the largest single producer and seller of rice. The Agriculture Minister herself was known to be an importer of rice." [11]

PAL urged the government to consider alternate proposals to raising the price of rice, but these were rejected by the government. PAL then sought permission from the government to stage a peaceful demonstration, but permission was denied. Liberians, however, began to gather for the demonstration anyway, leading the government to send its security forces to conduct a raid on PAL headquarters on the day of the demonstration, April 14, 1979. This action provoked a violent demonstration in the capital of Monrovia in which government soldiers opened fire on crowds of citizens and looting became rampant.

Afterward, PAL gained broad recognition and emerged as a new political party—the Progressive People's Party (PPP). On March 7, 1980, the PPP called for President Tolbert to resign. The government responded by arresting and imprisoning PPP leaders and members. Nevertheless, on April 12,

President William Tolbert and thirteen members of his cabinet were assassinated during the military coup of 1980.

The military government of Samuel K. Doe (with sunglasses) censored the press, executed political dissidents, and embezzled millions of dollars from the nation's treasury.

1980, Master Sergeant Samuel K. Doe led seventeen members of the Liberian armed forces, all of them indigenous Africans, in a military coup, executing Tolbert and thirteen key members of his cabinet. The coup leaders installed a new military government called the People's Redemption Council (PRC). The PPP and other political groups immediately declared their support for the PRC, and the PRC adopted many of the populist slogans used by these groups and even implemented certain reforms, such as abolishing some taxes on tribal leaders and improving some employment and housing conditions. However, the true nature of the new military government was soon revealed, as it employed violence, military repression, and corruption to stay in power and accumulate wealth.

For example, the new government assassinated scores of powerful, rich Americo-Liberians and looted and confiscated their property. President Doe also acquired a "loan" from the International Trust Company of Liberia to build a luxurious private house for himself, and distributed Mercedes Benz cars to his military officers. When students and academics began expressing concern about the new government, Doe raided the University of Liberia, killing, wounding, and arresting many students and staff. Doe also restricted press freedoms through terrorist acts such as the killing of journalists. Doe's policies brought the economy to a state of near collapse. Yet despite his corrupt and violent rule, Doe was able to obtain increasing amounts of U.S. military and economic aid during his rule, largely by aligning Liberia with U.S. positions on issues important to the United States in its Cold War with the Soviet Union. As military expert Major I.A. Nass explains, "Though obviously crude, corrupt and highly repressive, Doe's regime appeared to have been seen by [the] United States as having the capability to hold the Liberian state without antagonizing U.S. interests." [12]

In 1985, after intense Liberian and international pressure for a return to civilian rule in Liberia, Doe agreed to hold elections. Despite large voter turnout and wide opposition to Doe's rule, the government announced that Doe had won by 50.09 percent of the vote. Most Liberians, as well as outside observers, concluded that Doe had illegally fixed the result through voting irregularities such as the destruction of ballots, intimidation of voters, and improper supervision of the voting process. Doe thus became the civilian president of Liberia, but most of the population now hated his regime.

THE 1989 UPRISING

Shortly after the 1985 election, opposition rebels led by Thomas Quiwonkpa attempted but failed in a military coup to remove Doe. Quiwonkpa's Patriotic Forces fled into exile and joined with others to regroup and plan another attack on Doe. This attack came on December 24, 1989, when rebel forces, now called the National Patriotic Front of Liberia (NPFL) and led by Charles Taylor, entered Liberia from Côte d'Ivoire and began attacking and seizing towns in Nimba County, the southern part of the country. Doe sent troops to the area to contain the situation, but they could not stop the invasion. Instead, the rebel forces grew as many Liberians joined with the rebels to fight the government.

War raged between the army and the rebels, causing many deaths. Horrible atrocities were committed by both sides. Government troops reportedly killed innocent women and children without restraint, burying them in mass graves or dumping them at sea. Yet NPFL fighters also conducted their own ethnic cleansing, killing many who were believed to have supported Doe's rule. As Major I.A. Nass describes, "The Mandingo ethnic tribesmen, who were alleged to have co-operated with Doe's Krahn soldiers in the bloody raids in Nimba county during the two failed coups of 1983 and 1985, and Krahn ethnic groups were summarily executed in [the] hundreds." [13]

Rebel troops quickly gained the upper hand, acquiring control over most of the countryside. As a rebel victory appeared inevitable, government troops began deserting, and many citizens started fleeing Liberia by any means possible. Many called for Doe to resign, and Nigeria even offered him asylum. At first, in July 1990, Doe agreed to resign, then later changed his mind and decided to make his stand in Monrovia.

Soon thereafter, rebel troops reached Monrovia, the only Liberian territory still occupied by the government. At this stage, the rebel group NPFL broke into factions, creating a second rebel group called the Independent National Patriotic Front of Liberia (INPFL), which threatened to battle Charles Taylor's NPFL for control of Monrovia. The fight in Monrovia thus became a fierce, three-sided battle that created a state of anarchy in the capital city. All social and economic activities were halted, and civilians hid in their homes, afraid to venture outside even for food, for fear of losing their lives.

CIVIL WAR IN LIBERIA

In early August 1990, the leaders of a group of West African nations—called the Economic Community of West African States (ECOWAS)—met to discuss what could be done to stop the fighting in Liberia. These leaders, including the presidents of Nigeria, Ghana, Gambia, Guinea, and Sierra Leone and the foreign ministers of Togo and Mali, called for a cease-fire, created a peacekeeping force called the Economic Community Monitoring Group (ECOMOG), and planned to create an interim government that would eventually hold free elections in Liberia.

Upon hearing of the peacekeeping plans, President Doe and INPFL rebel leader Prince Yomi Johnson did not object.

LIBERIA'S CHILD SOLDIERS

Among the many atrocities committed during Liberia's civil war, experts say that as many as ten thousand children were recruited by both rebel and government forces to fight. Children as young as nine or ten were kidnapped from their homes or schools and forced to fight and kill using automatic weapons. Many of the children have taken part in killing, maiming, or raping of civilians, and many themselves have been killed or wounded. Reportedly, these child soldiers often became used to the idea of killing and destruction and in many cases turned into some of the most ferocious fighters during the war. This reaction is perhaps understandable given that the children were deprived of love and affection, beaten and treated badly by their kidnappers, and often given drugs to help them feel brave. Some were even forced to witness the execution of their family or friends, and were threatened with death if they screamed or cried. Rebel leaders liked the children because they followed orders more easily than adults, were more easily intimidated, and were considered dispensable. The United States and fifty-three other countries have signed a treaty setting the minimum age of combat troops at eighteen, but Liberia's fighters do not follow these rules.

Thousands of Liberian children fought on both sides during the country's civil wars.

However, Charles Taylor, leader of the NPFL rebel group, rejected the peacekeeping ideas, arguing that the Liberian crisis was an internal matter to be decided by Liberians without the interference of other countries. Taylor at this time was clearly on the verge of winning the war in Liberia; his group controlled almost 98 percent of Liberia, and indeed, he had already declared himself president of much of the country. Taylor threatened to resist any outside military or peacekeeping forces that might be sent into Liberia.

The West African countries ignored Taylor's threat and prepared a multicountry military force to move into Liberia. On August 24, 1990, a force of thirty-five hundred peacekeeping troops landed by sea in Monrovia and was welcomed by a jubilant crowd of starving and suffering civilians. The force fanned out across Monrovia and began the job of establishing order, clearing corpses, feeding civilians, and treating the sick and wounded. Within weeks, an interim government was set up, headed by Dr. Amos Sawyer.

Despite some initial successes, however, the West African peacekeeping forces allowed a serious breach of security that resulted in the death of President Doe. During the peacekeeping mission's third week in Monrovia, rebel leader Prince Johnson learned that Doe was planning to visit ECOMOG headquarters. Johnson staged an ambush that killed Doe's bodyguards and overwhelmed peacekeeping troops, and then brutally killed Doe by cutting off his ears, fingers, and genitals until he bled to death. As a result of this incident, peacekeeping forces improved their weapons arsenals and increased troop levels to six thousand. Also, peacekeeping troops went on the offensive, seeking to push all rebel forces out of Monrovia.

Peacekeepers brokered a cease-fire agreement in November 1990 between the leaders of the warring factions, but the agreement was broken by fighting soon after it was signed. Nevertheless, the West African peacekeepers doggedly continued their efforts for peace, organizing meetings of neighboring countries and rebel leaders, and constantly pushing for an end to the fighting and for free elections in Liberia. Various other peace accords were also signed, but each quickly collapsed amid more fighting. Meanwhile, Charles Taylor and his group of rebels maintained control of most of Liberia.

In 1992, peacekeeping troops decided to take on Taylor's rebel forces by deploying into NPFL-controlled areas of Liberia. Although Taylor pretended to cooperate, his fighters in reality offered significant resistance, at one point holding peacekeeping troops hostage for two weeks, creating an international incident. Peacekeepers also were forced to deal with other rebel groups, including a new group called the United Liberation Movement for Democracy (ULIMO), formed largely from former Doe government troops that earlier had fled into exile. Ultimately, West African peacekeepers withdrew and the situation in Liberia became highly unstable, even leading to a bold attack by Taylor's rebels on ECOMOG headquarters in Monrovia. There, the battle between rebels and peacekeeping troops raged for many months, until peacekeeping forces, with reinforcements, finally secured Monrovia and moved outward to capture several other areas, such as Monrovia's airport and nearby towns of Kakata, Harbel, and Buchanan. At that point, in April 1993, the peacekeepers halted military actions, to allow diplomatic peace talks to begin.

ECOMOG soldiers patrol the streets of Monrovia. Peacekeeping forces were involved in the civil war for three years before diplomatic talks began.

THE 1995 PEACE TREATY

As Taylor's rebels began losing territory to peacekeeping forces in the spring of 1993, Taylor called for the United Nations (UN) to intervene in the crisis in Liberia. Taylor wanted a cease-fire and for peacekeeping forces to include troops from outside the area of West Africa. Taylor believed the peacekeepers were dominated by Nigeria, which had supported President Doe and therefore lacked neutrality. Although many believed Taylor sought a cease-fire only to regroup for more fighting, the UN decided to become involved and assigned a special UN representative, Trevor Gordon Summers, to assess the situation. Summers and his team visited Liberia and met with peacekeeping forces and all the warring groups. While the United Nations was studying its options, however, Taylor broke the cease-fire that he himself had called for and staged another assault on ECOMOG positions. This was repelled only by massive tank, artillery, and mortar countermeasures.

Later that year, a UN-brokered peace agreement was signed, providing for a cease-fire, disarmament, and a new interim government council that would hold elections by February

THE WEST AFRICAN PEACEKEEPERS

Although the West African peacekeeping force, Economic Community of West African States (ECOWAS) is credited with effectively stopping Liberia's first civil war and setting up elections in 1997, some of its soldiers have been accused of looting and human rights abuses. According to press reports, ECOWAS soldiers from Nigeria sent into Liberia in the early 1990s stole items such as hospital equipment, motorcycles, and electrical cables and equipment, shipping them back to Nigeria for sale. In one incident, Nigerian peacekeepers pillaged an estimated $50 million worth of iron ore from a refinery. Worse, some Nigerian soldiers are said to have sold arms they had captured back to the rebel groups and skimmed profits off food aid sent to hungry Liberians. The ECOWAS soldiers apparently were extremely underpaid for their work, leading them to supplement their salaries by stealing.

Some of the same Nigerian troops were sent to Liberia in the summer of 2003 to begin another peacekeeping mission. Many observers fear that history will repeat itself because the soldiers' pay is still low and Nigeria has resisted attempts to correct the problems. Human Rights Watch in 2003 requested that peacekeepers entering Liberia be accompanied by advisers knowledgeable about humanitarian law, but there is no indication that the request will be considered or implemented by ECOWAS.

1994. Although elections were delayed, peacekeepers began disarming in March 1994, and humanitarian aid began to be distributed. However, as had often happened during Liberia's civil war, this peace treaty, too, ultimately failed amid continuing skirmishes between the various rebel groups. A coalition of new rebel groups attacked Taylor's headquarters, leading to a counterattack by Taylor's men and continuation of the civil war. As a result, elections were never held and the situation in Liberia deteriorated as more massacres were reported and civilians suffered.

Finally, in May 1995, the Nigerian government invited Charles Taylor to visit Abuja, Nigeria's capital. In the meeting, Nigeria sought and apparently achieved an understanding with Taylor in order to improve the peace process. Following the meeting, another peace conference was arranged to be held in Abuja in August 1995. At the Abuja talks, attended by all of the Liberian rebel groups, the UN and others pressured for an end to the civil war. The meeting resulted in the Abuja Accord I, which is considered a landmark in the Liberian peace process. This time, under the terms of the agreement, in addition to disarmament and free elections within a year, the leaders of the main warring factions were to form the interim government council. Its chairman was a professor of English literature from the University of Liberia—Wilton Sankawulop. The agreement was heralded in Liberia as an answer to everyone's prayers for peace.

THE ELECTION OF CHARLES TAYLOR

Not long after the new interim government was formed under the terms of Abuja Accord I, the rebel group ULIMO, led by Roosevelt Johnson, broke the cease-fire when different factions of the group began fighting with each other in northwestern Liberia. The infighting caused a split in the government council because representatives of the various rebel factions were represented there. There were rumors of secret shipments of arms to the rebel groups in Monrovia, and Charles Taylor used the crisis to assert more control. In March 1996, government forces controlled by Taylor, ignoring peacekeeping forces, tried to arrest rebel leader Roosevelt Johnson at his house in Monrovia in April 1996. The incident led to a breakdown of the cease-fire and to fighting between government forces, largely controlled by Taylor, and

Johnson's ULIMO rebels in Monrovia. The fighting later spread throughout the country.

The renewed fighting created yet another period of general insecurity and fear for civilians as the fighters looted and destroyed homes and property. In addition, fighters on both sides routinely engaged in inhuman practices against civilians. To give just one example, as described by Major I.A. Nass, "The fighters would bet over the sex of an unborn baby and subsequently cut open the stomach of a [live] pregnant woman, often of an opposing ethnic or factional group. They would bring out the unborn baby, make fun of it and kill it too."[14]

As a result of the deterioration in Liberia, West African countries of ECOWAS held another meeting in August 1996 in Abuja, Nigeria. The participants in the meeting decided that the 1995 accord remained the best hope for peace, but they decided to hold elections with or without total disarmament and to impose political sanctions on groups that violated the peace process. For example, violators would be prevented from participating in the elections process. In addition, peacekeeping forces were strengthened so they could deal more effectively with problems. Under the new schedule, rebel groups were directed to disband and disarm by January 1997, with elections to be held by the end of 1997.

Disarmament began slowly, and the United Nations became involved to help with humanitarian aid and with demobilizing rebel groups. Eventually, peacekeeping forces were successful in achieving disarmament of about 75 percent of the combatants. In February 1997, an election commission was organized and rebel leaders, including Charles Taylor, began preparing for elections. Taylor became the clear front-runner, but other candidates also emerged, including the only real challenger to Taylor—Ellen Johnson Serleaf, an official in the NPFL government and the first African woman to be elected to the UN Security Council. Elections were held on July 19, 1997.

Despite Taylor's history of brutality, Liberians desperate for peace elected him as president and gave Taylor's party an overwhelming majority in the Liberian legislature. He was seen as the only leader strong enough to end the civil war and stabilize the country. The voter turnout was high, there were no allegations of fraud or significant voter irregularities,

PRESIDENT CHARLES TAYLOR

Charles McArthur Ghankay Taylor was elected president of Liberia in July 1997. He and his National Patriotic Party ran Liberia's government until August 11, 2003, when he was pressured to resign and live in exile in Nigeria. One of seven children, Taylor was born on January 28, 1948, near Monrovia. His father was an Americo-Liberian and worked as a teacher, sharecropper, lawyer, and judge. His mother was a native Gola tribeswoman. As a young man, Taylor studied in the United States, at Chamberlayne Junior College and Bentley College, both in Massachusetts. He graduated with a bachelor of arts degree in economics in 1977.

While at college, Taylor became politically active protesting President Tolbert's policies. During President Tolbert's visit to the United States in 1977, Taylor led a demonstration against the president and was invited to debate Tolbert; he reportedly won the debate, but later was arrested. Tolbert generously decided not to press charges, however, and invited Taylor to return to Liberia. Taylor accepted and returned in 1980, just before the 1980 military coup. Taylor then became head of the General Services Agency in Doe's government, where he was in charge of purchasing for Liberia. Taylor was fired from this job in 1983, accused of embezzling more than nine hundred thousand dollars in government funds, and fled back to the United States. Taylor returned to Liberia in 1989 to lead a rebel force called the National Patriotic Front of Liberia (NPFL), which started the long period of civil war in Liberia, eventually overthrowing Doe's government and bringing Taylor to power. Taylor's record as Liberia's president is well known; he stole millions of dollars, fomented conflict in neighboring nations, and left the country in ruins.

President Charles Taylor resigned after his corrupt government was exposed.

and Taylor reportedly won with 75 percent of the vote. He was sworn in as Liberian president on August 2, 1997.

LIBERIA'S RENEWED CIVIL WAR

Charles Taylor's government faced overwhelming problems, including enormous domestic and international debt, tens of thousands of refugees with no housing or jobs, and a country whose capital, economy, and infrastructure had been virtually destroyed. The hope was that Taylor would seek reconciliation with his enemies, obtain foreign aid, and turn his energies toward reconstruction of the country. Quickly, however, this hope was dashed. Taylor largely appointed members of his rebel group, NPFL, to government posts, harassed the media, and formed his own army made up of NPFL fighters.

Taylor's government, like the Doe regime before it, became known for its corruption and brutality. As the Associated Press describes, "Charles Taylor used fear, patronage and state monopolies to control what diplomats and business leaders estimate amounted to 90 percent of Liberia's economy—everything from imported rice to diamonds, timber and lucrative shipping registry fees." [15] He used the revenues from these national resources for his own personal benefit, stashing as much as $1 billion in Swiss bank accounts. In addition, as a 1999 report from the U.S. Department of State described, "the Government's human rights record was poor, with serious problems in many areas." [16] Indeed, Taylor's state security forces terrorized Liberia; they closed newspapers and threatened journalists, extorted money from citizens at roadblocks, and arbitrarily killed many people, particularly those from ethnic groups or tribes that had opposed Taylor during the civil war.

Taylor then began destabilizing neighboring countries. In 1999, Ghana, Nigeria, the United States, and Britain accused Taylor of arming a rebel group called the Revolutionary United Front in the neighboring country of Sierra Leone in exchange for diamonds. The rebels deposed Sierra Leone's president in 1997 and began a campaign of terror against civilians suspected of supporting the president, creating a flood of about 250,000 refugees who fled to Guinea, joining the many thousands of refugees there from Liberia. The president of Sierra Leone was returned to power in 1998, but

Liberia continued to support the rebel Sierra Leone forces. In 2000, Britain intervened to support UN peacekeeping troops, ending the violence. In 2003, Taylor was indicted by Sierra Leone's UN-backed tribunal for war crimes and violations of international humanitarian law during Sierra Leone's civil war. The court called for Taylor's arrest and extradition to Sierra Leone to face criminal charges.

The rebellion supported by Taylor in Sierra Leone also spread to other neighboring countries. In April 1999, Taylor accused Guinea of supporting Liberian rebels from ULIMO, who attacked the Liberian town of Voinjama, displacing more than twenty-five thousand people. Guinea, meanwhile, claimed that Liberian forces were entering its territory and attacking its villages. Unrest also began in Côte d'Ivoire. In 2002, a military rebellion there was led by the Ivory Coast Patriotic Movement, a group supported by Liberian fighters. In 2002, France sent troops into Côte d'Ivoire to secure a cease-fire and end the civil war there. The United States and others called on the UN to impose sanctions against Liberia for its involvement in fomenting rebellion in West Africa.

Taylor's actions in these other African countries helped create support for two new Liberian rebel groups opposed to Taylor's government, leading to yet another brutal civil war in Liberia between these rebel groups and Taylor's government forces beginning in 1999. The first of these rebel groups— Liberians United for Reconciliation and Democracy (LURD)— largely comprised members of the Mandingo tribe and was backed by Guinea and Côte d'Ivoire. Another group—the Movement for Democracy in Liberia (MODEL)—was dominated by Krahn tribesmen and was also supported by Côte d'Ivoire. The renewed fighting killed tens of thousands and forced more than a million Liberians from their homes. In 2003, MODEL advanced in southern and eastern Liberia while LURD fighters from the north pushed closer and closer to Monrovia, eventually laying siege to the city. Both government and rebel troops, by this time, were unpaid, often only children, who freely looted and plundered Liberia whenever fighting broke out. Attempts to negotiate a cease-fire between the warring groups proved fruitless, and in early 2003 pressure mounted for an international peacekeeping force to be sent to Liberia. Eventually, peacekeepers arrived and Taylor fled the country, but the once-prosperous nation had been shattered.

4

THE SOCIETY OF LIBERIA

The most defining social and political influence in Liberia is its mix of different ethnic groups. One ethnic group, called Americo-Liberians, comprised freed American slaves who settled and founded the country. Multiple other indigenous ethnic groups, or tribes, make up the balance of Liberia's population. Americo-Liberians became the social and political elite in Liberia, excluding from power most people of tribal backgrounds for much of Liberia's history. This created, essentially, two separate societies, one settler and the other tribal. Eventually, however, this inequality was challenged by indigenous Liberian groups, leading to the end of Americo-Liberian domination, and ultimately, many believe, to the country's current state of anarchy, poverty, and war.

AMERICO-LIBERIAN SOCIETY

According to Liberian historians, the group of Liberians that became known as the Americo-Liberians actually was made up of three different classes. The first was a class of light-skinned black settlers from America who formed the country's early power elite. This class was considered the highest status level, and it controlled the social, economic, and political life of the country during its first decades. During this period, light skin color was considered the prerequisite for participation in the highest levels of Liberia's government and society. The second class comprised the rest of the black settlers from America and their descendants. The third class was called the Congoes, the name given to persons who were rescued from slave ships caught operating in African waters. By 1860 the number of Congoes in Liberia was about equal to the number of settlers in the country. As a result, the Congoes were accepted into the Americo-Liberian group. As these three groups began to intermarry in the late 1800s, skin color became increasingly unimportant as a badge of social and political status in Liberia, and darker-skinned Americo-Liberians came to power.

Nevertheless, Americo-Liberians drew distinctions between themselves as a group and the great mass of tribal people native to the area of West Africa called Liberia. These indigenous Africans called the settlers *kwi,* and Americo-Liberians began using this term to mean "civilized" because they considered themselves superior to the native Liberian tribal people. The degree of one's *kwi* within the Americo-Liberian group depended on criteria such as family background, education, and church membership. Tribal people could become *kwi* only in cases of adoption or intermarriage with Americo-Liberians and only by assuming American or European names, getting a Western education, and adopting Americo-Liberian customs and culture.

A freed American slave poses after arriving in Liberia. The native tribes of Liberia came to resent Americo-Liberians, who evolved into the country's political elite.

During most of the first century of Liberia's nationhood, Americo-Liberians lived separately from Liberia's native tribes and the two groups rarely even had meaningful contact. The settlers, or Americo-Liberians, had brought with them from America many Western values and customs, and they lived primarily near Monrovia, Liberia's capital, and along the coast. Indigenous people, on the other hand, had their own distinct cultures and lived autonomously, mostly in the interior areas of Liberia, referred to as the Hinterland. For many decades, very little economic interaction occurred between the two groups. For the most part, Americo-Liberians participated in a market economy—that is, producing products and trading with other countries—while tribal Liberians largely worked in a subsistence economy—growing only enough food to feed their families and survive.

Notably, Americo-Liberians formed a very small part of Liberia's total population—only about 2 to 3 percent. Indeed, the upper classes of Americo-Liberians that formed the political and social elite of the country during its early years numbered only about two thousand people, all of whom lived in or around Monrovia. They went to the same churches, joined the same clubs, and went to the same schools and universities. They spoke only English and they intermarried. Several social organizations also cemented the bond among the Americo-Liberian elite, particularly the Ancient, Free, and Accepted Masonic Lodge of Liberia. Members of this group often became leaders in Liberia. Indeed, as a Library of Congress study notes, "Five presidents of the republic, beginning with Roberts [Liberia's first president], were brand masters of the [Masonic] order, which came to be seen as the repository of community ideals and the symbol of Americo-Liberian solidarity."[17]

INDIGENOUS ETHNIC GROUPS AND LANGUAGES

The native Africans who lived in the part of West Africa that became Liberia are believed to have come originally from the Niger Plateau to the north, from the regions south of the Gambia River to Angola. Some of the earliest tribes in the area, for example, were the Kpelle and Gola. Later, other tribes migrated from the northern Ivory Coast area, including Kru, Bassa, Dey, and Grebo. In addition, Muslim tribes such as the Vai and Mandingo arrived from Sudan.

LIBERIA'S SIXTEEN TRIBES

Although they were similar in some ways, Liberia's sixteen tribes—Mende, Gola, Gbandi, Loma, Kissi, Mandingo, Geh, Mah, Kpelle, Bassa, Krahn, Grebo, Kru, Vai, Dey, and Belle—also had their differences. For example, the Mandingo were a mix of Arab and Sudanese Negro blood and were largely responsible for developing the group of languages of inner West Africa. Tribes from northern and central Liberia, such as the Gola, Dey, and Bassa, were known for their bold demeanor. The Gola and Dey were also known for cultivation of large farms of rice and cassavas (grown for its starchy root). The Bassa and the Kpelle tribes were the largest tribes, and the Bassa tribe, which lived closer to the coast, quickly accepted the education and Christianity that the settlers offered, and sent many of their sons to Western schools. The Kru, another coastal tribe, was powerful and warlike, and its men became great fishermen and seamen. Indeed, Kru were hired to work on merchant ships from many different nations, allowing them to travel widely and learn to be good traders as well. The Grebo tribes, in southern Liberia, were similarly known to be proud and warlike. The Vai tribe was the most advanced intellectually; they invented their own alphabet and written language. Today in Liberia, many people from these tribes have moved, intermarried, and adopted Western customs, creating a very diverse society. Nevertheless, identifiable tribal groups still exist, as can be seen in the groups fighting in the country's civil wars.

Liberia has officially categorized the tribal people into sixteen tribes: Mende, Gola, Gbandi, Loma, Kissi, Mandingo, Geh, Mah, Kpelle, Bassa, Krahn, Grebo, Kru, Vai, Dey, and Belle. Many of these tribal categories, however, are somewhat arbitrary and not based on clear criteria such as a common language, a recognized territory, a distinctive culture, or political/social cohesion. For example, under this system, the southeastern Kruan-speaking people, although they spoke the same language, were separated into three separate tribes (Grebo, Kru, and Krahn). Nevertheless, generally speaking, the Gola, Dey, and Vai tribes occupied the northern part of Liberia; the Bassa, Kru, and Grebo tribes were found in the south; and the Kpelle were from central Liberia. The Vai, Dey, Bassa, Kru, and Grebo lived near the coasts, while the Kpelle, Krahn, Kissi, and others occupied the interior areas. Other tribes, such as the Mandingo, simply cannot be categorized geographically because they lived in various parts of Liberia. The two largest tribes are the Kpelle and Bassa.

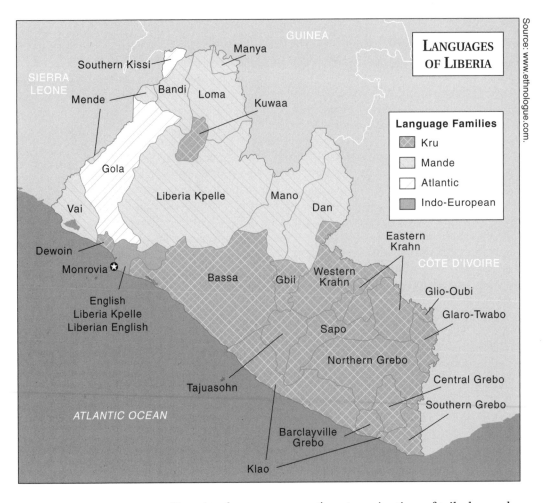

Despite the government's categorization of tribal people, the reality was that indigenous people did not see themselves as members of tribes. Indeed, the traditional everyday life of indigenous Liberians was governed less by identification with a particular ethnic or tribal group than by kinship ties within their village or a small group of villages. For example, among the Kru tribe, the largest political unit was the *dako,* which was made up of several villages of persons linked by male ancestors. However, as native people began to interact with Western people and companies, they often began to identify themselves more as a member of a tribe in order to fit into Western perceptions and acquire jobs and benefits. For example, the Kru earned a reputation among early European traders for being good port workers, and many people identified themselves as Kru in order to obtain work. In addition, after the Americo-Liberians began to lose power, politicians and those seeking power or government benefits identified with a particular tribe mainly to emphasize their tribal roots and distinguish themselves from the Americo-Liberians.

In addition, although English is the official language in Liberia, tribal people speak a wide variety of different tribal languages. These native languages can be divided into three main language categories—Mande, Kru, and West Atlantic. However, each of these categories can be further divided into subcategories, each of which will then have several dialects. The Kpelle, for example, speak five different dialects of the same language. Further, the tribal languages, and even the dialects, are very distinct from one another. Only two tribal languages have an alphabet and can be written—Kpelle and Vai. As a result of living among so many languages, most Liberians speak several languages fluently. Also, over the years, tribes have commingled, moved from one geographic area to another, and made adaptations to many twentieth-century influences. As a result, Liberia's population today is truly a mixture of various cultures and customs.

TRIBAL SOCIAL AND POLITICAL STRUCTURES

Traditional tribal social structures in Liberia were based on family or kin relationships between people residing in the same village or group of villages, called a chiefdom. In many cases, the members of a chiefdom were related by common ancestors. The chiefdoms typically were small, most with fewer than five thousand people. Within the chiefdom, status was linked to how directly one was related to the founding ancestor, and the eldest male with the highest status often became the chief. In some tribes, however, power and status came not from ancestry but rather from wealth and military abilities. For example, certain tribes that became involved in slave trading in the eighteenth and nineteenth centuries awarded chiefdoms and power to warriors as a reward for their loyalty and military successes.

The chief functioned as both priest and king, leading religious rituals and, with the aid of tribal government councils, governing the chiefdom and dispensing justice in civil matters and punishment for all crimes. The chief held this position for life in most cases. Although different from the type of governments in more developed societies, as Dr. C. Abayomi Cassell describes, "these [tribal] governments functioned smoothly and effectively."[18]

By the 1900s, tribal status became linked largely to wealth, which was defined not in terms of possessions but rather in terms of how many people one controlled. This wealth was derived largely from a tribal custom called "pawning," in which an adult could lend himself or a dependent (often a child) to another in exchange for money or some other payment. The pawn would then work for the other person until he or she was redeemed. A person's wealth would be based on the number of pawns he controlled. This practice became common in Liberia.

Another form of wealth was based on the number of wives, cattle, and dependents one had. Wives were particularly important because they produced the offspring. For example, in the Kpelle tribe, a man with many wives would be considered a rich man and have better living conditions than others. He was called a *to nuu,* or in English, a "big shot." Such a rich man, or big shot, would be expected to help others less fortunate in his village. He would help feed others, often lend his wives to other men in the village, and provide protection. In exchange, villagers would offer their loyalty.

Yet another part of tribal social structure included initiation or membership in a number of organized associations dedicated to traditional African education, spiritual matters, and culture. Two important examples, utilized by at least ten of Liberia's sixteen tribes, are the Poro (for males) and Sande (for females) societies. In the Poro society, which might be compared to the Masons in Americo-Liberian society, boys were trained to become useful and law-abiding men and leaders. In Sande, girls were trained in the domestic arts, handicrafts, singing, and dancing. For those tribes that subscribe to this practice, all members of the tribe were eligible to join. Indeed, initiation in these organizations was considered a necessary part of becoming a full-grown man or woman, and those who were not properly initiated were prohibited from participating in much of the tribe's political and ritual activities. Although modern educational opportunities and work culture have weakened the influence of Poro and Sande, both groups remain part of Liberian society even today.

PORO AND SANDE SOCIETIES

Poro and Sande are organizations that provide religious, social, cultural, and practical instruction to youngsters from many of Liberia's tribes. Although sometimes called secret societies, because only members are permitted to be present for their meetings or rituals, these organizations were actually the tribal equivalent of Western schools and the Americo-Liberian Masonic order. Indeed, they were often called traditional or bush schools, and they provided not only skill training but also a social, religious, and cultural identity to indigenous people. For example, boys would be trained by Poro and girls by Sande in adult skills such as hunting, farming, healing techniques, music, dance, and religion. This training was extensive, continuing for many years. Such training and initiation into Poro or Sande was, at one time, considered necessary for indigenous Liberians to graduate into adulthood. Thereafter, initiates remained members of the societies and could achieve various ranks within the society based on seniority and knowledge. High-ranking Poros were given great respect among Liberian tribes. The Liberian government was at first hostile to Poro and Sande, viewing them as pagan groups. During President Tubman's administration, however, they became protected organizations, and Tubman himself became the official head of Poro in 1964. Today, Poro and Sande are recognized as cultural societies in Liberia and, with the availability of Western education and jobs, have become less important to traditional Liberians than they once were.

Liberian girls celebrate their acceptance into a secret tribal society with special costumes and body art.

RELATIONS BETWEEN AMERICO-LIBERIANS AND TRIBAL LIBERIANS

From the beginning of Liberia's history, the Americo-Liberians held themselves apart from indigenous tribes, whom they considered to be barbaric. Indeed, Liberia was established for the American settlers, and its founders did not give much consideration to the indigenous African population. Liberia's constitution in 1847, for example, specifically stated that the purpose of the country was to provide a home for "the dispersed and oppressed children of Africa,"[19] which meant black settlers from America. Also, the constitution limited citizenship to "persons of Negro descent," a term that was interpreted in practice to refer only to Americo-Liberians. This meant that people from Liberian tribes who had lived in the area for centuries were not granted legal citizenship in their own lands.

Instead, these indigenous people (called "aborigines" by Americo-Liberians) were referred to only briefly in the constitution and given only vague promises that their lands would be protected and that the government would promote their advancement. In the end, neither of these promises was kept. Indeed, citizenship was not clearly granted to tribal people until the election of the William V.S. Tubman in the mid–twentieth century. Americo-Liberians built a society and economy separate from that of native peoples, and the politics and social life of the new country were dominated completely by Americo-Liberians for over a hundred years. As historian Tom W. Shick describes, "In reality what the settlers chose to view as a nation was in fact two distinct and unequal societies—one settler, the other African."[20]

Understandably, from the time of the first settlements of Americo-Liberians, there was conflict between the settlers and African tribal groups, as the new government sought to exert its power over local people. Much of the conflict in the beginning was caused by the settlers' attempts to prevent coastal tribes such as the Kru and Grebo from trading slaves with slave ships that came to Liberia's coasts, a practice the tribes had engaged in for centuries. These tribes repeatedly attacked Americo-Liberian settlements during the 1800s, sometimes threatening their very existence. One common tactic used by the tribal groups was cutting off the settlers' trade and supplies of food; early settlers often had to call on the U.S. Navy to help them break these embargoes.

As the republic became more established, Americo-Liberians explored farther and farther into Liberia's interior. These explorers established new trading relationships with inland tribes and made treaties with local chiefs for protection or for the purchase of tribal lands. In this way, the government's influence was slowly expanded into the interior of Liberia—the Hinterland. Tribal people, however, resented these intrusions, particularly the idea of settlers purchasing their land. According to tribal customs, tribal chiefs did not even have the power to dispose of tribal lands, because territories occupied by tribal people were not owned by individuals but were shared communally, by all members of the tribe. Also, the land purchases often displaced large numbers of locals from lands they had lived on for centuries. By the early twentieth century, the government began to collect taxes from tribal people and impose restrictions on the power of their chiefs, causing more conflict between settlers and indigenous people.

There were even reports that government officials had forced aborigines to perform forced labor or slavery, an ironic and sad development, since the government was itself run by descendants of former African slaves. Indeed, the government's bad treatment of tribal groups became known abroad and resulted in criticism of the Liberian government, leading to the creation of an international commission to investigate the matter. The commission's 1931 report confirmed that aborigines in Liberia were used as slaves and implicated many high-level government officials in this practice. The slavery scandal resulted in the resignation of Liberia's president and in great embarrassment for the country. It is viewed as a stain on the country's history even today.

THE RISE OF INDIGENOUS LIBERIANS

The economic growth of industries such as rubber, iron ore, and diamonds demanded both skilled and unskilled labor, and attracted many tribal people into the cities, the plantations, and the mines. The process began with the establishment of the Firestone rubber plantation in the 1920s, which employed tens of thousands of tribal Liberians as wage earners for the first time in the country's history. Additional economic opportunities were created as a result of U.S. investment during

Firestone plantation workers transport buckets of rubber. Firestone was the first foreign company to establish operations in Liberia.

World War II and President Tubman's Open Door Policy. The establishment of new businesses and industry, in turn, fostered the building of new roads and railroads into the Hinterland, providing improved access to the area and further increasing contact between rural native populations and the settler class. Many missionaries built schools for outlying tribes, providing some indigenous children with a Western education. By the 1950s and 1960s, the country was in the middle of an economic boom, which brought a degree of wealth and education to Liberians from every ethnic group. By 1977, it was estimated that about 160,000 native Liberians were working for wages, compared with 30,000 in 1950.

These changes disrupted traditional tribal culture and village life and exposed tribal people to Western ways. For example, although initially many indigenous workers quit their jobs after short periods to return to their tribal homes, they later became permanent employees, and their families often moved near the plantations or mines and shared their salaries. In addition, throughout the 1900s, native Liberians moved to urban areas, such as Monrovia, where they were free from traditional tribal responsibilities and customs and forced to adapt to Western culture and learn English. These urban Liberians were aided in this transition by the establishment of voluntary tribal associations, such as the Kru Corporation and the Organization of Grebo Market Women, which provided aid and support to tribal Liberians. As a result, some tribal customs and kin-based connections continued to be important.

The economic changes also allowed Americo-Liberians and native Liberians to interact, and intermarriage between the two groups became common. These intermarriages brought more people of tribal background into the Americo-Liberian world of status, education, and power. President Tolbert's mother, in fact, was a member of Liberia's Vai tribe. By the late 1900s, as historian Stephen Ellis notes, "there had been such extensive interaction, political, social and sexual, between people of settler and 'tribal' origin that the governing elite was already thoroughly infiltrated by people of country origin." [21]

In addition, the economic changes paved the way for greater involvement by indigenous groups in Liberia's political life. As people of tribal backgrounds acquired a measure of education and economic freedom, they became more aware of the social and political inequalities existing in the country. Finally, in the 1970s, the economy became depressed, decreasing opportunities and increasing prices for the struggling tribal masses, heightening their growing dissatisfaction with the government. As a result of these and other factors, groups of educated indigenous Liberians formed to protest the inequities, eventually leading to the downfall of the Americo-Liberian ruling class.

Indeed, the ethnic divide provided the backdrop for the country's 1980 military coup. Doe, himself a descendant of the Krahn tribe, claimed to be redeeming Liberia from the minority rule of Americo-Liberians. The government, overnight, was taken over by soldiers of tribal background and by people who had criticized the Americo-Liberian domination of the country. The coup leaders arrested hundreds of elite Americo-Liberians and looted or confiscated their property. The Grand Lodge that housed the Masonic order in Monrovia and which had become a symbol of Americo-Liberian rule was attacked and burned, and Masonic meetings were banned. The period of America-Liberian dominance thus gave way to rule by Liberians claiming to represent indigenous people.

However, some America-Liberians, who were educated and technically competent, were needed in Liberia's modernized economy, and they continued to hold important positions in postcoup Liberia. As a result, a new class of educated, technically trained Liberians of varied or mixed ancestry emerged.

THE MASONIC LODGE OF LIBERIA

Prior to the 1980 coup, political, social, and economic power were focused in a small, elite group of America-Liberian families. This upper class lived in and near Monrovia and attended the same schools, churches, and social clubs. Probably the most important of these clubs, or fraternal orders, was the Ancient, Free, and Accepted Masonic Lodge of Liberia. Founded in 1867, the Masonic order produced many of the True Whig Party leaders of Liberia. The chapter located in Monrovia was called the Grand Lodge, and reportedly, many important ideas affecting the nation were discussed and decisions made within its walls. For Liberians of tribal background, the Grand Lodge thus became a symbol of the minority control exercised by the America-Liberians and the tribal peoples' lack of access to politics. As a result, after the 1980 coup, the Masons were outlawed for a while. During Liberia's civil wars, the Grand Lodge was burned and damaged by numerous battles. However, some loyal Masons have expressed a desire to restore the Grand Lodge.

Burned and damaged, the Masonic Lodge in Monrovia stands next to a piece of artillery.

Some were Americo-Liberians, but many others were mixed blood, with only one Americo-Liberian parent, or one parent of tribal backgrounds. Unfortunately, many of these educated Liberians fled the country to escape Liberia's civil wars.

THE ROLE OF INTERTRIBAL DISPUTES IN LIBERIA'S CIVIL WAR

Although most of Liberia's tribes did not engage in the fighting, Liberia's long civil war essentially was a struggle between several tribal groups vying for power in postcoup Liberia. In the first phase of civil war during the Doe administration, for example, four of Liberia's sixteen tribes fought for power. Supporting the Doe government were the Krahn and Mandingo tribes, while the Gio and Mano tribes backed Taylor's rebel group. Both sides engaged in attacks that targeted civilian members of opposing tribes. In one incident, for example, Doe's troops slaughtered six hundred Gio and Mano civilians seeking asylum inside St. Peter's Lutheran Church in Monrovia.

Later, groups that organized to oppose Taylor's government—LURD and MODEL—were largely made up of fighters from the same Mandingo and Krahn tribes, many of them ex-members of Doe's government forces. Once again, Taylor's government troops and these rebel groups committed terrible atrocities on civilians believed to be members of the opposing tribes. War in Liberia became less a battle for liberation or empowerment of the masses of indigenous Liberians and instead simply a battle between certain tribes for power and control.

Unfortunately, when one side gained power in Liberia, that power was used corruptly, to benefit only that leader and members of his tribal groups. Some see this corruption as an outgrowth of the traditional African custom to provide for and protect those related to him. As journalist Anthony Daniels explains, "In Africa . . . [a man] enriches himself not only for his own sake, but for . . . a number of concentric social circles that radiate from him and of which he is the chief ornament: his family, his village, his tribe, and so on." [22] The problem with this approach is that it completely excludes those who are not part of the tribe or tribes who are in power, condemning many to poverty and leading others to rebel against the government, creating another round of civil war. Having finally achieved access to power in Liberia, the indigenous people have yet to find a leader who will govern the whole of the country effectively.

5

LIFE AND CULTURE IN LIBERIA

Although Liberia's elite, at least before the recent civil wars, lived a modern urban life similar to Western societies and influenced by Christian values, much of Liberia's population remained poor and influenced heavily by tribal customs and values. For example, those in the upper echelons of business and government, perhaps only about 2 percent of the population, were very well off with housing and material goods comparable to their counterparts in the United States. Most Liberians, however, continued to live traditional tribal ways and in poverty, without modern conveniences or material goods. The same division between elite and tribal cultures can be seen in other areas of everyday life, such as education, religion, food, dress, and culture. However, the interaction between elite and country people in Liberia has begun to produce a society in which the values and customs are a mixture of influences.

HOUSING

Housing in Liberia can be divided into three main styles. First, along the coast, particularly in cities such as Monrovia, beautiful frame houses are built in what is described as colonial or plantation style, similar to houses one might find in the southeastern United States. These houses typically have two stories, a stone basement, and wood framing, a portico on both the front and back. This style was used by the settler classes when they first founded the country, and today these buildings are still used and occupied by those considered to be the country's social and political elites.

The second style of housing can be described as traditional tribal dwellings. This style consists of mud huts and is found largely in the interior Hinterland. The huts are built by using sticks as walls, filling the spaces between the sticks with mud or clay, and plastering the outside with a finer material such as cow droppings. Thatched roofs are typically formed from palm leaves. Some tribes build round huts, while others are square or rectangular, and sometimes the rectangular ones use corrugated tin roofs.

Yet a third type of housing can be found in the urban areas, where an influx of people during the country's economic boom resulted in the building of cheap slum housing. Since then, the government has helped to construct additional, decent housing for many thousands. These buildings typically are constructed of cement blocks with corrugated tile or metal roofs. Many skilled and unskilled workers occupied this type of housing, at least until the recent civil war. The war, however, has destroyed many of Liberia's public and private buildings, creating a housing crisis in the country.

Many Liberian villagers live in traditional mud huts with thatched roofing like these.

HEALTH AND WELFARE

Like many aspects of Liberian life, the quality of health care is distinctly divided along social lines. Hospitals and the best health care facilities are located largely in the cities and therefore are more accessible to the more elite and educated Liberians. Rural Liberians, however, must rely on traditional healers and small health clinics set up by the government. In the 1960s and 1970s the government built a number of these rural clinics.

Even before civil war erupted in the country, however, limited funding slowed the building of adequate facilities and negatively affected the quality of health care available in the country clinics. During the course of the war, all Liberia's hospitals and clinics have been destroyed and their medical supplies looted. Aid workers beginning to move into Liberia in 2003 discovered large numbers of people in need of urgent medical care.

For example, International Medical Corps (IMC), an international nonprofit group specializing in providing medical care and humanitarian aid, visited the town of Bensonville soon after the area had been secured by peacekeepers. According to IMC's report, at a clinic it set up in the town, "within a three and a half day window, the team treated close to 500 patients, of which 37 percent were under the age of five.

AIDS IN LIBERIA

In addition to the traumas caused by civil war, health experts warn of another health danger to Liberians. As of 2001, more than 17 million Africans have died from the AIDS/HIV virus, and Liberia appears to be part of this trend. A 2001 Central Intelligence Agency (CIA) estimate indicated that 2.8 percent of the adult population of Liberia between the ages of fifteen and sixty-four are infected with human immunodeficiency virus (HIV), the virus that causes AIDS. This amounts to 51,298 people, most of whom are between the ages of fifteen and twenty-nine. Also, experts say traditional infectious diseases in Liberia, such as malaria, yellow fever, and cholera, will increase the rate of death among HIV-infected Liberians because their immune systems are weakened by AIDS. Since 2001, more Liberians have tested positive for the virus, and the infection rate appears to be rising. The government of Charles Taylor did little to combat the AIDS threat. In September 2003, however, the World Health Organization announced plans to provide drugs for AIDS treatment to 3 million people by the end of 2005.

Malaria presented in more than 51 percent of the patients, as well as a significant number of respiratory tract infections, diarrhea, and skin diseases."[23]

EDUCATION

Historically, Liberia's educational system has also been divided between the elites and the masses. The Americo-Liberian settlers established public primary and secondary schools for their children early, along with various church-supported schools and institutions of higher education. Liberia College, for example, was founded in 1863 in Monrovia and now is called the University of Liberia. The oldest of the vocational schools is the Booker Washington Institute. In addition, children of the Americo-Liberian elite were often sent abroad to schools in Europe or the United States for the best possible education.

The ruling classes, however, had little interest in providing education to the country's indigenous population during this period. Instead, children from the various tribes attended traditional tribal "bush schools" run by the Poro and Sande societies. Children attended these schools for four to seven years and learned skills useful for living in tribal society, such as hunting, farming, domestic arts, music, and dance. Some native Liberians also attended Muslim religious schools. Quite a few schools were established by missionaries in the late 1800s and early 1900s in the Hinterland, but the instruction was limited to primary education and only a limited number of local Liberians were reached by these efforts. As a result, only Americo-Liberians were truly educated during the first century of Liberia's existence.

During the Tubman and Tolbert administrations, however, efforts were made to improve education for more Liberians. As a result, the government school system was reorganized to provide kindergarten for children aged four and five, six years of elementary school for children aged six to twelve, junior and senior high schools, and postsecondary education. Also, during the 1950s, 1960s, and 1970s, new elementary and secondary schools were built, and primary and secondary education was provided for free. As a result of these changes, the numbers of students in primary and secondary schools increased dramatically. Many indigenous children were also sent to the bush schools, but the time spent there was reduced to only about a year. The educational advances allowed greater numbers of indigenous people to attain an education.

Despite these improvements, however, only a little more than half of Liberia's children attended school in 1980. In addition, the quality of the instruction at Liberian schools was low. Although a large percentage of the national budget was spent during certain years on education, schools were not properly funded, and as a result could not attract good teachers or pay for textbooks or other basic materials such as blackboards and erasers. When civil war broke out, funding became even more scarce, many schools were destroyed, and the chaos of war disrupted Liberia's education program completely. As of 2000, about eighty percent of the population still was unable to read and write.

As for postsecondary schools and colleges, as of 1984 there were three main ones: the University of Liberia in Monrovia, the country's oldest college; Cuttington University College in Suakoko, a college run by the Episcopal Church with government subsidies; and the William V.S. Tubman College of Technology, founded by the government in 1978. The University of Liberia was the largest and most prestigious college; by 1981 it enrolled more than three thousand students and offered curricula in liberal arts, business, science and technology, agriculture and forestry, medicine, and law. Cuttington University College was a smaller school, specializing in economics, education, and nursing. The Tubman College of Technology was the newest school with the smallest enrollment of students, but it offered degrees in engineering technology, and specializations in civil, mechanical, electrical, and electronic engineering and in architecture. These schools, however, have all been damaged or destroyed by war.

WORK

In part due to the educational divide, elite educated Liberians historically held the best, highest-paying jobs while lower-skilled, lower-paying jobs went to Liberians of tribal ancestry. Early Americo-Liberians held jobs in government, commerce, and large-scale agriculture. Traditionally, most of the tribal people of Liberia were farmers, and many still work in agriculture, tilling crops to feed their families and villages. A few exceptions to this rule include the Bassa tribe, whose members focused less on farming and more on hunting and gath-

ering of forest products, and the coastal Kru, who became able sailors and fishermen. In contemporary times, many indigenous people have moved to cities, towns, or other areas where businesses have been established, finding work in the various industries that make up Liberia's economy. Eventually, after the divide between elite and native Liberians faded, more educated Liberians of tribal backgrounds began working in government and other higher-prestige, higher-paying jobs.

Less than half of Liberian children attended school in 1980. Today, even fewer children are likely to receive a comprehensive education.

When Liberia's economy began to deteriorate in the 1970s as a result of the worldwide recession, Liberia saw high levels of unemployment. After the 1980 coup, under the Doe and Taylor administrations, the economy declined even further and poverty and unemployment became widespread. Both presidents raided the national treasury while the people suffered. In addition, the series of civil wars that Liberia experienced virtually decimated the country's economy. The fighting destroyed most of the country's buildings, infrastructure, schools, and businesses, and many educated and technically trained Liberians fled into exile in other countries.

Also, the UN Security Council voted in March 2001 to impose sanctions on Liberia in retaliation for Charles Taylor's support for rebels in neighboring Sierra Leone. The sanctions, which were renewed in 2002, blocked all diamond sales by

Although Liberia's civil wars destroyed many businesses, small business owners like this owner of a gas station are able to eke out a small living.

Liberia, banned the import of Liberian timber, restricted international travel by top Liberian officials, and prohibited the shipment of arms to the country. The effect of the sanctions was to further damage Liberia's economy, work opportunities, and the standard of living for Liberians. As of 2003, an alarming 85 percent of the Liberian population was unemployed and living below the poverty level, which is set at one U.S. dollar per day.

RELIGION

One's religion in Liberia was also a function of one's social background—that is, whether one was from an elite or tribal background. Tribal religions and traditional African beliefs once accounted for the majority of belief systems in Liberia. Although there were differences, most tribal religions were similar in that they were based on the worship of ancestors and the idea that spirits of the dead have access to a higher God and influence over the daily lives of living persons. From this idea, tribal religions developed various rituals used to make offerings to the spirits, to pacify them or gain their assistance with some earthly matter. If the spirits were pleased, one could expect worldly success; if the spirits were angry, sickness and misfortune were likely. In addition, followers of tribal religions often carried with them objects, called amulets or charms, for protection and strength. Today, these tribal beliefs are less strong than in the past, weakened by the growth of other religions and the advance of modern culture. However, many people still rely on magical objects or amulets and seek out tribal spiritual advisers, called *zos*, for assistance.

Christianity came to Liberia first as part of Americo-Liberian society. The Liberian constitution guaranteed freedom of religion and prohibited religion from being used as a test for civil office. All of the major Protestant denominations in the United States gained a foothold in Liberia, with the Methodists and the Baptists the largest, but also including the Episcopalians, Congregationalists, and Presbyterians. Most of this early Protestant religion was conservative and evangelical, emphasizing emotional revival meetings to convert sinners to accept Christ as the son of God. Prior to the military coup in 1980, membership in a Christian church was considered a necessity for holding political office. By the mid- and later 1900s, however, church and religion were not as important in Liberia, and church attendance among the nontribal population had declined.

Once foreign missionaries were permitted into the interior of Liberia, they built schools and tried to convert what they viewed as the "heathen" tribal Liberians to Christianity. Early missionaries, however, had difficulties because they did not know tribal languages and viewed tribal culture and religion as incompatible with Christian beliefs. For example, Christians insist on monogamy (in which a husband has only one wife), while polygamy (the practice of having many wives) for native Liberians was part of their system of wealth and status. In some cases, missionary groups tried to learn local languages and tried to accommodate local customs wherever possible. As a result of these missionary activities, many people from Liberian tribes have converted to Christianity. Also, it is not uncommon for Christian beliefs to be combined with selected tribal beliefs.

In addition, about 10 percent of the Liberian population is Muslim—that is, followers of the Islam religion. African Muslims believe in one God, called Allah, but also in the existence of spirits created by that God, thus accommodating local tribal beliefs. Muslims also pray five times every day: at dawn, just before noon, before sunset, after sunset, and at night. In addition, for one month each year, the month of Ramadan, Muslims must abstain from sexual relations and fast from sunrise to sunset. Another requirement is the giving of alms, or help, to others and making a trip to the holy city of Mecca.

FOOD AND CLOTHING

Further divisions between elite and tribal cultures can be seen in other areas of everyday life, such as food and dress. Before the war, Liberia's best hotels and restaurants served a variety of American, European, and other international foods. However, more typical West African fare is often found in roadside restaurants, known as "cookhouses," where dishes, usually rice with traditional toppings made from various local ingredients, are cooked on outside hearths.

For example, these cookhouses might offer Jollof Rice, a rice dish made with tomatoes and spices, together with cabbage cooked with bacon and pigs' feet, sweet-potato leaves with fish, or palm nuts with shrimp in fish or chicken stock. Other dishes include Check Rice, a mixture of rice and okra, and goat soup, which is considered the national soup. Pies and sweet desserts are popular, and ginger beer and palm wine are the common drinks. Other typical foods found in markets include the leaves and starchy roots of the tropical cassava plant, small hot red peppers, sweet potatoes, yams, plantains, collard greens, cabbage, eggplant, okra, coconut, fresh ginger, and fresh fruits such as mangoes and oranges. The staple food is rice, which is eaten twice a day in most households.

The dress in Liberia tends to be casual. Although early settlers and the elite Americo-Liberians favored formal attire similar to that worn in the United States, and Western clothing is still popular, especially among Liberia's educated classes, traditional clothing or a mixture of the two is more common. Also, the heat in Liberia usually dictates that clothes be made of cotton. A typical traditional outfit for a woman, for example, might be a cotton dress, or blouse and skirt, with a *lapas*, or piece of cotton cloth, wrapped around the waist and tied. Women often also wear colorful cotton scarves around their heads. For men, the common dress is cotton short-sleeved shirts and pants, or for more formal wear, a "swearing in suit," which has a loose-fitting, colorful pullover top and matching pants. Many people go barefoot.

A boy picks cassava leaves. The large roots and leaves of the plant are common ingredients in Liberian recipes.

LIBERIAN SOLDIERS IN WIGS

One of the more shocking images of Liberia's civil war was the sight of government and rebel soldiers sporting wigs and wearing women's clothing, along with their automatic weapons. Although it looked bizarre to Westerners, this type of cross-dressing is actually a military tactic that indigenous Liberians use to make themselves feel protected and make their enemies fear them. The cross-dressing is rooted deeply in West African traditional cultures, where medicine men or religious leaders recommend wearing masks as a way of increasing one's power. In addition, in Liberian initiation rituals, boys often are encouraged to wear female clothing as part of the process of graduating into manhood. The Liberian soldiers, often still boys, who dress in women's gowns and wigs are simply practicing a modern version of these traditions, trying to look as powerful and fearsome as they can to gain military advantage on the battlefield.

In keeping with ancient tradition, a rebel soldier dresses as a woman as a means of intimidating the enemy.

ART AND CULTURE

In the fields of art, music, and dance, the settler-tribal division is very evident. Descendants of the settler class were largely influenced by the culture of southern America of the nineteenth century, with slight contributions from contemporary Western and traditional African ideas. For example, literature in Liberia began in the late nineteenth century with the first Americo-Liberian novel, *Love in Ebony,* written by Charles Cooper. Other writers and poets followed, some in more recent years seeking to integrate traditional storytelling and folktales with Western literature.

Indigenous Liberians, meanwhile, had their own distinct and diverse culture, which in recent decades has been recognized as a national treasure worth preserving. Perhaps the most important indigenous cultural expression is found in traditional music and dance rhythms, which typically involve the use of drums and percussion instruments. Each tribe developed its own ritual dances and music to celebrate important events. The drumming requires great skill, and drums range from huge war drums to so-called talking drums, in which the drummers change the pitch as they play by tightening or loosening the drumheads. The beat of the drums is often accompanied by other instruments, such as reed rattles, bells, horns, or types of string instruments. In addition, some tribes such as the Kru have a tradition of vocal music or choirs.

Traditional tribal dances are also an important part of Liberian culture. President Tolbert encouraged the development of native culture, and under his administration a National Culture Troupe was created to perform plays and dances based on traditional Liberian themes, both at home and abroad. The Poro and Sande societies also have played a large role in preserving many of these musical and dance traditions.

Another Liberian tradition is mask carving. Masks are used in Poro and Sande religious and social rituals. Often made from sapwood, the masks employ different styles, from very lifelike masks to ones with grotesque human or animal features, such as beaks or horns. Other items, such as utensils, figurines, or ceremonial pieces, are also carved from the wide variety of local hardwoods and other materials, such as soapstone and clay. A variety of additional traditional crafts can also be found in Liberia, including weaving, jewelry, and cloth making. Many modern Liberian art pieces, following traditional styles, tend to be abstract rather than representational. Liberian art and crafts can be seen at the National Museum in Monrovia, as well as locations such as the National Culture Center near Monrovia, which contains a cultural village showing huts from each Liberian tribe together with traditional arts and crafts.

Contemporary popular culture tends to be a mixture of Western and traditional influences. In urban areas, for example, nightclubs feature bands playing music known as highlife, a style similar to Caribbean or South American music, which is a blend of Western and African rhythms.

A woodcarver sculpts a piece of wood into a statue. Most Liberian handicrafts follow traditional tribal designs.

RADIO, TV, AND NEWSPAPERS

From the beginning of Liberia's existence, newspapers were important in the settler community. The country's first news publication, for example, was the *Liberia Herald,* founded in 1826. Many other newspapers flourished thereafter, until the Doe and Taylor governments in the late 1900s cracked down on press freedoms and closed many news publishers.

For indigenous Liberians, however, many of whom are unable to read and write, radio and television became the most important forms of communication. Before the recent civil wars, seven radio stations, including a Voice of America station, and one television station broadcast within the country.

In contemporary Liberia, however, President Taylor's government shut down several independent radio stations, such as Star Radio and the Catholic Church–owned Radio Veritas, and sought to dominate the media with the Liberian Communication Network (LCN), a communications company owned by Taylor and his party. LCN operated a television station, two FM radio stations, and one shortwave radio station. It also owned a printing press and published two newspapers. Prior to Taylor's departure, Liberia's press, television, and radio broadcasts were almost completely taken over by the government; only a few small independent voices remained.

Communications, therefore, as with many other aspects of Liberia's life and culture, has been greatly affected and disrupted by the many years of war and violence. Life in Liberia will only get back to normal once the fighting stops for good.

6

A Chance for Future Peace

Liberians finally achieved a shaky peace in August 2003, when Charles Taylor was forced to leave the country and the two main rebel groups signed a peace agreement providing for elections in October 2005. West African peacekeepers, backed by a few American marines, spread into Liberia to keep the fragile peace. A reduction in the fighting was expected to allow humanitarian groups to begin addressing the overwhelming food and medical needs. It will take much longer, however, for the country to heal from fourteen years of civil war, which not only destroyed the country's economy and infrastructure, but also killed tens of thousands, tore apart families, and uprooted them from their homes.

Taylor Steps Down

In June 2003, warring groups in Liberia finally signed a cease-fire, but within a week the cease-fire was shattered as rebel fighters moved into Monrovia. On June 26, 2003, U.S. president George W. Bush called on President Taylor to resign. With Liberia and Monrovia in chaos, Taylor finally agreed to resign as soon as peacekeeping troops arrived.

Pressure built for the United States to intervene and take a lead role in a peacekeeping mission in Liberia, and in July 2003, President Bush announced that U.S. troops would be sent to help the West African countries of ECOWAS stabilize the country. Bush explained, however, that the U.S. action would be limited, to allow humanitarian aid to take place and prepare for the situation to be turned over to UN troops in short order.

On August 4, 2003, the first small contingent of a West African peacekeeping force (this time called ECOMIL or ECOMIL's Mission in Liberia) arrived in Monrovia. That same day, twenty-three hundred U.S. marines also arrived, taking a position on American warships off the coast of Liberia. The rebel group, LURD, promised to work with the peacekeepers. Finally, on August 11, 2003, Charles Taylor resigned and began his exile in Nigeria.

A PEACE ACCORD

On August 14, 2003, peacekeeping forces, accompanied by about 200 U.S. troops, arrived in Liberia and were greeted by

DEMONSTRATIONS FOR PEACE

As the world debated how to deal with the crisis in Liberia in the early summer of 2003, Liberian refugees trapped in the capital city of Monrovia held demonstrations outside the U.S. embassy there, begging the United States to send help. In some cases, the demonstrators vowed to go on hunger strikes; in other cases, they piled up dead bodies to make their point about the need for international assistance. Meanwhile, Liberian women and children refugees living in the neighboring country of Côte d'Ivoire demonstrated there, claiming that they were harassed by fighters and by local inhabitants of Côte d'Ivoire. They demanded that they be evacuated immediately and returned to their homes in Liberia, a difficult demand given the ongoing fighting there. When West African and American troops finally arrived in Monrovia, they were swarmed with crowds of joyful Liberians in a warm welcome. Liberians were clearly sick of war.

Liberian women demonstrate for peace in front of the U.S. embassy in Monrovia.

Crowds cheer as peacekeeping forces roll into Monrovia in early August 2003. Peacekeeping forces put an end to the fighting and established an interim government.

thousands of cheering Liberians. The rebel forces of LURD, led by Abdullah Sherrif, withdrew from Monrovia, peacefully handing over control to the peacekeepers. Within two weeks, peacekeeping forces in Liberia quickly grew to 3,250 soldiers after reinforcements from Ghana, Senegal, and Mali arrived. General Festus Okonkwo, commander of the peacekeeping troops, explained, "ECOMIL is not here to fight anybody, it is not here to kill anybody, and it is not here to be killed by anybody."[24] Instead, he said, the peacekeepers' purpose was to remove weapons and militias from Monrovia, including the government forces established by former president Taylor. The ECOMIL and American forces quickly secured the capital of Monrovia, and promised to hand over control of the military and political operation to a UN force in October 2003.

Soon thereafter, on August 18, 2003, Taylor's government, led by Taylor's vice president, Moses Blah, and the two warring rebel groups, LURD and MODEL, signed a peace treaty. The accord officially ended Liberia's civil war and created a new interim government that would prepare for free elections to be held in two years. The rebel group LURD demanded to be appointed to the vice chairmanship in the interim government, but treaty mediators refused to concede this point. Under the terms of the treaty, therefore, none of the three warring factions (Taylor's forces, LURD, and MODEL) would be appointed to the interim government. Instead, only neutral noncombatants were to form the new interim government.

Despite the peace treaty, fighting still continued in the countryside. By early September 2003, the peacekeepers had largely restored calm to Monrovia and announced they would move into other parts of Liberia. Their first major deployment was to be in the area near the town of Kakata, just thirty miles north of Monrovia. However, reports of rebel fighting in the area postponed ECOMIL's deployment, and when peacekeeping troops were sent to the area to investigate, they found that the rebel group LURD had already captured the town. The continued fighting sent fifty thousand new refugees fleeing toward Monrovia. ECOMIL fortunately was able to secure Kakata and drive the rebels out, and its forces slowly began the process of clearing Liberia of fighting, one town at a time. As of the early fall of 2003, ECOMIL had gotten off to a good start, but it was too soon to tell whether ECOMIL's peacekeeping mission would be a complete success.

The Interim Government

On August 21, 2003, businessman Charles Gyude Bryant was appointed to lead the interim government. Bryant was chosen from a list of candidates submitted by civil and political groups, and was considered the most neutral candidate. Besides running a successful heavy equipment company, Bryant is a member of the indigenous Grebo ethnic group, a pillar of the Episcopal Church, and a virtually unknown political figure in Liberia. He explained that he sees himself as a healer for Liberia: "I see myself as neutral. I side with no group. I'll strive to bring the opposing factions together. We need to heal our country, to end the retribution and to see that the basic rights of the people are ensured." [25]

Bryant, who will be called chairman rather than president, took over from Vice President Moses Blah on October 14, 2003, and will govern until 2005, when elections are to be held. Many questioned allowing Blah to remain in control of

Liberia, because of his close ties to Charles Taylor; both had fought together against the Doe government. However, Blah was known as a quiet man without much political ambition, and he handed over power in October and promised to do what it takes to bring peace to Liberia.

Officials such as Jacques Paul Klein, the UN special representative for Liberia, urged the United Nations to adopt a strong mandate for Liberia—one that would allow it to disarm and demobilize all warring groups. The UN goals then would be to conduct a census, register citizens for political parties, build a grassroots political process, and conduct an election. Chairman-elect Bryant pledged to work closely with the United Nations to achieve these goals.

THE HUMANITARIAN CRISIS

By the time peacekeeping troops arrived in the country, Liberians were desperate for food and humanitarian assistance. Indeed, just before ECOMIL arrived in Monrovia, desperate Liberians—men, women, and children—attacked Monrovia's port, tearing open sacks of food shipped there for distribution by ECOMIL, looking for something to eat. Rebel fighters fired their guns into the air in an attempt to control the mob until ECOMIL forces arrived.

Carolyn McAskie, a senior UN humanitarian official sent to Liberia, said that the humanitarian situation was grim: "The situation on the ground is very desperate here in Monrovia. . . . We are very concerned about the large number of displaced but also the people in their homes who have no access to food." [26] The humanitarian aid process, she indicated, would take a minimum of two years. Hundreds of thousands of Liberians continued to live in makeshift refugee camps in and around Monrovia, because they were forced to flee their homes to escape the fighting between rebels and Taylor's government forces. In Monrovia alone, the refugee population grew by at least three hundred thousand when people from the countryside swarmed into the city in June 2003 as a result of the rebel offensive to oust Taylor. Another refugee camp, located about fifty-six miles from Monrovia in Salala, swelled from thirty thousand to fifty thousand refugees as a result of fighting after the signing of the peace accord. Aid workers in such camps in September were trying to decide how to distribute high-energy bars

CHARLES GYUDE BRYANT, LIBERIA'S INTERIM LEADER

In August 2003, Liberia's president, Charles Taylor, resigned and international peacekeepers moved into the country to establish peace between the fighting groups. The West African peacekeeping group set up an interim government to take charge as of October 2003 and appointed Charles Gyude Bryant as the chairman of that government. Bryant was selected largely because he was seen as neutral in his politics. Indeed, very little is known about him. He is fifty-four years old, was born in Monrovia, and in 1972 earned a graduate degree in economics from Cuttington University College, a Liberian college.

Two years later he married Rosielee Williams and they had three children. His wife works for United Airlines in the United States. Bryant is not descended from American ancestors, but rather from the Grebo tribe. He is chairman of the Episcopal Church of Liberia. He also is a businessman who runs a heavy equipment company that supplied much of the machinery for Monrovia's port. Bryant has promised to try to heal Liberia, and unlike leaders in Sierra Leone who conducted a war crimes tribunal after that country's civil war, he wants to give amnesty to all persons involved in Liberia's civil war with one exception—ex-president Charles Taylor.

Chairman Charles Gyude Bryant has pledged to bring peace to his troubled country.

and other food to these large numbers of people without causing mass riots.

In addition to the lack of food and water, Liberia's population faced the dangers of diseases such as cholera and dysentery, particularly in Monrovia. Humanitarian workers warned that an outbreak of cholera could quickly spread in the unsanitary conditions created by the rebel attack on the capital. Clinics in the city reportedly had been treating up to 350 cholera patients per week until they were closed by rebel

FINDING LOST CHILDREN

Liberia's civil war separated many thousands of children from their families. In August 2003, after the ouster of President Charles Taylor and the arrival of peacekeeping troops, the Red Cross was able to began to operate a family tracing program that sought to reunite these lost children with their parents. The Red Cross maintains an office in Monrovia, Liberia's capital, where it has a list of the names of more than fourteen hundred of these children, from infants to teenagers. The agency, with the help of Radio Veritas, a Roman Catholic broadcast service in Liberia, broadcasts the names of children and any information about them, hoping that their families will hear the radio program and come for them. As *New York Times* journalist Tim Weiner reported in an article on August 22, 2003, entitled "Liberia's Split Families Heal, Child by Lost Child," the program is resulting in some successes. For example, the program reunited Krubo Toe, a small, scared girl of twelve, with her mother, Comfort Toe. Mother and child were separated when rebels attacked their town of Bopolu, in northern Liberia, about eighteen months earlier. According to Weiner, Mrs. Toe wept with relief and said, "This war has taken everything."

A woman scans Red Cross photographs of children separated from their families during the civil war.

forces. In addition, the city's only water treatment plant was destroyed in the attacks, making sanitation even more of a problem.

In the interior parts of Liberia, the situation was even worse. Reportedly, people there were still dying, either from starvation, disease, or war wounds, and many continued to survive only by eating wild cassava roots. Aid workers hoped to get aid to the countryside as soon as those areas could be secured by ECOMIL. In mid-September, UN workers began this process by trucking refugees from Monrovia back into the countryside. Aid workers also began making tentative trips into the still insecure countryside to assess humanitarian needs; initial reports were that malnutrition and disease were rampant.

ECOMIL troops made a priority of securing Roberts airfield, Liberia's main airport, as well as Monrovia's seaport. These were expected to be used to bring in the vast quantities of humanitarian assistance that Liberia desperately needed. Yet the humanitarian task ahead for Liberia was daunting. A World Food Program official, Ramin Rafirasme, summed up the challenge faced by the beleaguered nation: "It's going to take years of work and thousands of peacekeepers to secure this country."[27]

PSYCHOLOGICAL DAMAGE

Perhaps the most destructive part of the fourteen-year civil war was the damage done to families and children as the fighting brought death and destruction to all parts of Liberia. Estimates for the number of Liberians killed in the war have run as high as three hundred thousand. The 2003 rebel assault on Monrovia alone, for example, killed approximately two thousand just before the peace treaty was signed. Also, it is estimated that almost 1 million Liberians have been displaced by the civil war; this amounts to about one-third of the country's total population.

In addition, the war tore apart hundreds of thousands of families and destroyed everything they owned. When rebels or government troops attacked and looted villages, they took food and possessions at will. Women and children, even boys, were often raped. Many villagers were simply killed. Children or other family members were often lost in the confusion and separated from their families as villagers ran to escape the violence. Some lost children ended up in refugee camps alone or were taken in by other families or clinics. As soon as the peace treaty was signed, the Red Cross, an international humanitarian group, began trying to locate Liberia's lost children and reunite them with their families with the help of Radio Veritas, Liberia's only functioning radio station.

Many unlucky children, however, faced an even worse fate when they were captured by rebel or Taylor's government troops and forced to fight against their will. Indeed, as of August 2003, as many as ten thousand children remained trapped as fighters for government and rebel forces. These children were placed in what were called "Small Boy Units," made up of children as young as ten. As Dr. Peter Coleman, the Liberian minister of health and social welfare, described, "In some areas they [the child soldiers] are 40 to 50 percent of the fighting force. Young people with arms has become a way of life." [28] The psychological impact of forcing children to kill and maim their own people has yet to be fully investigated or understood, and Liberia has no social services or public health facilities to treat or rehabilitate these children.

The damage done to these child soldiers was multiplied when many of them were persuaded or forced to take drugs to help them fight. Tons of cocaine were shipped to Liberia throughout the 1990s, and both rebels and government troops gave the drug to young fighters to make them feel brave and fearless. Dr. Edward Grant, a Liberian psychiatrist, believes this drug abuse added to the horrors of war for Liberian children: "These children are the most dangerous segment of the fighting machine. . . . They have been used to commit atrocities under the influence of drugs." [29]

LIBERIA'S CRIPPLED ECONOMY

The civil war and Taylor's corrupt government also destroyed most of Liberia's economy and infrastructure. As a result of the fighting and instability, many businessmen fled the country, causing a drain of capital and expertise. Cities, towns, and villages throughout Liberia were almost completely decimated. In addition, almost all roads, bridges, and railroads were destroyed in the war, along with the country's electrical grid, water treatment plants, and communication services. Even the capital city of Monrovia no longer had electricity or water at the end of the civil war. As Liberian exile Ezekiel Pajibo puts it, "Today . . . [Liberia is] a prostrate nation, on

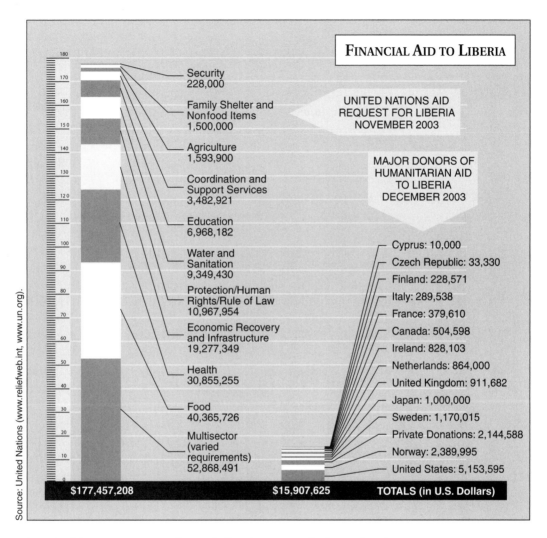

Source: United Nations (www.reliefweb.int, www.un.org).

FINANCIAL AID TO LIBERIA

UNITED NATIONS AID REQUEST FOR LIBERIA NOVEMBER 2003

Security 228,000

Family Shelter and Nonfood Items 1,500,000

Agriculture 1,593,900

Coordination and Support Services 3,482,921

Education 6,968,182

Water and Sanitation 9,349,430

Protection/Human Rights/Rule of Law 10,967,954

Economic Recovery and Infrastructure 19,277,349

Health 30,855,255

Food 40,365,726

Multisector (varied requirements) 52,868,491

MAJOR DONORS OF HUMANITARIAN AID TO LIBERIA DECEMBER 2003

Cyprus: 10,000
Czech Republic: 33,330
Finland: 228,571
Italy: 289,538
France: 379,610
Canada: 504,598
Ireland: 828,103
Netherlands: 864,000
United Kingdom: 911,682
Japan: 1,000,000
Sweden: 1,170,015
Private Donations: 2,144,588
Norway: 2,389,995
United States: 5,153,595

$177,457,208 $15,907,625   TOTALS (in U.S. Dollars)

bended knees—our pride and dignity severely brutalized. Liberia, once the beacon of hope in Africa, an oasis of peace, is now [an] Africa eyesore."[30]

Taylor not only failed to repair the economic damage but also is believed to have stolen much of the country's wealth. Although Liberia is endowed with water, mineral resources, forests, and a climate favorable to agriculture, Taylor did not use these resources to improve the country or pay for public projects. Instead, throughout his administration, he used Liberia's revenues to reward his political cronies and to enlarge his own personal bank accounts. Thanks largely to Charles Taylor, Liberia, although once prosperous, became an impoverished nation, unable to feed its people or support itself economically.

For Liberia to recover, its infrastructure must be rebuilt and jobs must be created to give people incomes. These goals depend on the development of sound economic policies that will encourage foreign investment, as well as on generous support from the United Nations and other countries. The economy of Liberia will quite literally have to be rebuilt from the ground up—a difficult job of nation building that will cost hundreds of millions of dollars. No one knows, however, exactly where these funds will come from.

In addition, experts say that it will be important to keep Charles Taylor from maintaining control over Liberia's economy from his exile in Nigeria. In September 2003, there were already reports that Taylor was violating the terms of his exile agreement by making repeated telephone calls to Vice President Blah and Liberian foreign minister Lewis Brown. He also was reported to be trying to raise funds by collecting debts from Liberian business figures in Monrovia and soliciting donations. Nigerian president Olusegun Obasanjo warned Taylor against these types of activities, stating that "the conditions given and accepted by Mr. Taylor for his asylum in Nigeria clearly forbid any interference in the outgoing political process . . . in Liberia."[31] In addition, UN officials announced that Taylor stole $3 million from Liberia as he fled into exile. The money, which would be enough to run Liberia for six months, was donated to Liberia by Taiwan to help with the peacekeeping process. Whether any of these monies could be recovered and returned to Liberia to help with its rebuilding was not certain as the peacekeeping process began.

U.S. AND INTERNATIONAL ROLES

It remains to be seen how much the international community will help Liberia, or what role the United States is willing to play. Soon after the cease-fire began, a small team of UN officials was dispatched to Liberia to coordinate with the peacekeeping forces. In September 2003, the UN Security Council approved the sending of 15,000 troops, 1,115 international police, 250 military observers, and 160 staff officers to the war-ravaged nation. This UN peacekeeping force was the largest troop deployment in UN history and was expected to include troops from many different countries, including Russia, the European Union, and the United States. The United Nations operation took over the peacekeeping function from the West African peacekeeping forces on October 1, 2003.

UN envoy Jacques Paul Klein also planned to organize a conference of international donors in Paris to help raise money for rebuilding the country. Initial estimates of the amount of aid needed in Liberia were $68 million. As of September 2003, half of this amount had been raised, primarily from the United States, Britain, and other European countries. Many, however, expected that this estimate could easily rise to $100 million. Funds are expected to be used to pay for roads, hospitals, and electrical grids, to rebuild the port of Monrovia, and to pay ex-combatants to give up their weapons.

Klein and many others also strongly urged the United States to stay in Liberia to help with reconstruction. Indeed, because of the special relationship between the United States and Liberia, many urged America to take the lead in reconstruction there, similar to the way Britain and France did with their respective West African allies, Sierra Leone and Côte d'Ivoire, following civil wars in those countries. With assistance from these Western powers, both Sierra Leone and Côte d'Ivoire managed to successfully rebound from the ravages of war.

The United States, however, busy with nation building in Iraq and Afghanistan, seemed unwilling to take a prominent role. In fact, although it agreed to provide $20 million in reconstruction aid, the United States on August 25 pulled most of its troops out of Liberia, leaving only about one hundred soldiers to guard the U.S. Embassy and act as liaisons with West African peacekeepers. The American pullout disappointed many Liberians, who saw it as a desertion by the country it considers its most important ally. These remaining U.S. troops left on October 1, just before the interim government was scheduled to take power. The United States was expected to continue to maintain a low profile, contributing relatively small amounts for reconstruction aid and dedicating its efforts in Liberia to well-defined projects such as trying to build a new Liberian army.

LIBERIA'S FUTURE

Although Liberia clearly needs humanitarian aid and international funding, its future also largely depends on Liberians themselves. No one can forget that the last peacekeeping mission resulted in the people legitimately electing the brutal rebel leader Charles Taylor as president. This time, Liberians are urging that members of the rebel groups not be permitted back into government, at least not until they have completely disarmed. In addition, ideas to solve the problems facing Liberia include dealing with corruption by paying government officials properly, implementing a government code of conduct, and taking actions to ensure that Charles Taylor

With international attention focused on Liberia at the end of the civil war, Liberians now have cause to hope for a brighter future.

cannot bribe or otherwise influence legislators. Others have proposed enforcing total disarmament and pacification of the country, or in other words, removing all weapons and abolishing the army, keeping only a police force.

Some also emphasize the need for Liberians to handle reconstruction themselves, rather than relying on international forces. They add that it is important for refugees to be returned from other countries, both to provide the expertise that many of them could bring to the new Liberia and to give all Liberians a chance to vote in the upcoming elections and a stake in building a new country.

Overcoming the challenges Liberia faces will not be easy. Nevertheless, Liberians at last had reason to hope for the first time in fourteen years, as Taylor was finally removed from power, as peacekeeping forces appeared to be making progress in ending the fighting, as humanitarian aid was beginning to be sent to the country, and as international attention finally was being focused on Liberia's needs. Despite the many questions still looming for Liberia, it at least now looks forward to a chance at peace and the possibility for a better future.

FACTS ABOUT LIBERIA

GEOGRAPHY

Location: Western Africa, bordering the North Atlantic Ocean, between Côte d'Ivoire and Sierra Leone

Area: 43,000 square miles total (land: 37,189 square miles; water: 5,811 square miles)

Area comparative: Slightly larger than Tennessee

Border countries: Guinea, Côte d'Ivoire, Sierra Leone

Coastline: 359 miles

Climate: Tropical; hot, humid; dry winters with hot days and cool to cold nights; wet, cloudy summers with frequent heavy showers

Terrain: Mostly flat to rolling coastal plains rising to rolling plateau and low mountains in northeast

Natural resources: Iron ore, timber, diamonds, gold, hydropower

Land use: Arable land, 1.97 percent; permanent crops, 2.08 percent; other, 95.95 percent (1998 estimate)

Natural hazards: Dust-laden harmattan winds blow from the Sahara (December to March)

Environmental issues: Tropical rain forest deforestation; soil erosion; loss of biodiversity; pollution of coastal waters from oil residue and raw sewage

PEOPLE

Population: 3,317,176 (July 2003 estimate)

Age structure: 0–14 years: 43.4 percent (male 724,960; female 716,831); 15–64 years: 53 percent (male 858,191; female 898,851); 65 years and over: 3.6 percent (male 59,539; female 58,804) (2003 estimate)

Population growth rate: 1.67 percent (2003 estimate)

Birth rate: 45.28 births/1,000 population (2003 estimate)

Death rate: 17.84 deaths/1,000 population (2003 estimate)

Infant mortality rate: 132.18 deaths/1,000 live births

Life expectancy: Total population: 48.15 years; male: 47.03 years; female: 49.3 years (2003 estimate)

Fertility rate: 6.23 children born/woman (2003 estimate)

Ethnic groups: Indigenous African tribes 95 percent (including Kpelle, Bassa, Gio, Kru, Grebo, Mano, Krahn, Gola, Gbandi, Loma, Kissi, Vai, Dei, Belle, Mandingo, and Mende); Americo-Liberians 2.5 percent (descendants of immigrants from the United States who had been slaves); Congo people 2.5 percent (descendants of immigrants from the Caribbean who had been slaves)

Religions: Indigenous beliefs 40 percent, Christian 40 percent, Muslim 20 percent.

Languages: English 20 percent (official), some twenty ethnic group languages, of which a few can be written and are used in correspondence

Literacy rate for those age fifteen and over: Total population, 57.5 percent; male, 73.3 percent; female, 41.6 percent (2003 estimate)

GOVERNMENT

Country name: Republic of Liberia or Liberia

Form of government: Republic

Capital: Monrovia

Administrative divisions: Fifteen counties; Bomi, Bong, Gparbolu, Grand Bassa, Grand Cape Mount, Grand Gedeh, Grand Kru, Lofa, Margibi, Maryland, Montserrado, Nimba, River Cess, River Gee, Sinoe

National holiday: Independence Day, July 26 (1847)

Constitution: Adopted January 6, 1986

Legal system: Dual system of statutory law based on Anglo American common law for the modern sector and customary law based on unwritten tribal practices for indigenous sector

Suffrage: Eighteen years of age; universal

Executive branch: Charles Gyude Bryant leads an interim government until elections can be held in 2005; cabinet is appointed by the president and confirmed by the Senate; president is elected for six-year, renewable term

Legislative branch: Bicameral National Assembly consists of the Senate (twenty-six seats; members elected by popular vote to serve nine-year terms) and the House of Representatives (sixty-four seats; members elected by popular vote to serve six-year terms)

Judicial branch: Supreme Court

Political parties and leaders: Alliance of Political Parties (a coalition of LAP and LUP); All Liberia Coalition Party (ALCOP); Liberian Action Party (LAP); Liberian People's Party (LPP); Liberia Unification Party (LUP); National Patriotic Party (NPP); United People's Party (UPP); Unity Party (UP)

Flag: Eleven equal horizontal stripes of red (top and bottom) alternating with white; there is a white five-pointed star on a blue square in the upper hoist-side corner; the design was based on the U.S. flag

ECONOMY

Gross domestic product (GDP): $3.5 billion (2002 estimate); real growth, -5 percent (2002 estimate); GDP per capita, $1,100 (2002 estimate); GDP composition, agriculture 74 percent, industry 7 percent, services 19 percent (2001 estimate)

Labor force: Agriculture 70 percent, industry 8 percent, services 22 percent (2000 estimate)

Industries: Rubber processing, palm oil processing, timber, diamonds

Agriculture products: Rubber, coffee, cocoa, rice, cassava (tapioca), palm oil, sugarcane, bananas, sheep, goats, timber

Exports: $110 million (2002 estimate)

Imports: $165 million (2002 estimate)

Debt: $2.1 billion (2000 estimate)

Economic aid: $94 million (1999)

Currency: Liberian dollar (LRD)

NOTES

CHAPTER 1: A TROPICAL PLACE

1. Voice of America, "Reduction in West Africa's Rainforests," October 24, 1996. http://forests.org.
2. C. Abayomi Cassell, *Liberia: History of the First African Republic.* New York: Fountainhead, 1970, p. 404.
3. Thomas D. Roberts et al., *Area Handbook for Liberia.* Washington, DC: Foreign Area Studies, American University, 1972, p. 278.

CHAPTER 2: LAND OF THE FREE

4. Cassell, *Liberia: History of the First African Republic,* p. 10.
5. Quoted in Cassell, *Liberia: History of the First African Republic,* p. 13.
6. Cassell, *Liberia: History of the First African Republic,* p. 89.
7. Quoted in Cassell, *Liberia: History of the First African Republic,* p. 130.
8. Quoted in Roberts et al, *Area Handbook for Liberia,* p. 14.
9. Quoted in Cassell, *Liberia: History of the First African Republic,* p. 191.
10. Quoted in G.E. Gaegbe Boley, *Liberia: The Rise and Fall of the First Republic.* London: Macmillan Education, 1983, p. 44.

CHAPTER 3: LIBERIA AT WAR

11. Major I.A. Nass, *A Study in Internal Conflicts: The Liberian Crisis and the West African Peace Initiative.* Nigeria: Fourth Dimension, 2000, p. 35.
12. Nass, *A Study in Internal Conflicts,* p. 59.
13. Nass, *A Study in Internal Conflicts,* p. 61.
14. Nass, *A Study in Internal Conflicts,* p. 158.

15. Associated Press, "Liberia's Taylor Won't Give Up Empire," *New York Times,* September 8, 2003.

16. U.S. Department of State, Bureau of Democracy, Human Rights, and Labor, "Liberia Country Report on Human Rights Practices for 1998," February 26, 1999. http://pages. prodigy.net.

CHAPTER 4: THE SOCIETY OF LIBERIA

17. Library of Congress, Federal Research Division, *Liberia: A Country Study,* ed. Harold D. Nelson, 1985. www.global security.org.

18. Cassell, *Liberia: History of the First African Republic,* p. 391.

19. Library of Congress, Federal Research Division, *Liberia: A Country Study.*

20. Tom W. Shick, *Behold the Promised Land.* Baltimore, MD: Johns Hopkins University Press, 1980, p. 142.

21. Stephen Ellis, *The Mask of Anarchy.* New York: New York University Press, 1999, p. 284.

22. Anthony Daniels, "Big Men, Big Corruption: The Way It's Done on the (Not So) Dark Continent," *National Review,* August 11, 2003.

CHAPTER 5: LIFE AND CULTURE IN LIBERIA

23. International Medical Corps, "International Medical Corps Expands Health Care Services to Communities Outside Monrovia," September 8, 2003. www.imcla.com.

CHAPTER 6: A CHANCE FOR FUTURE PEACE

24. Quoted in Tim Weiner, "Peacekeepers Take Liberia, Foot by Foot," *New York Times,* August 18, 2003.

25. Quoted in Tim Weiner, "A Man Without Enemies," *New York Times,* August 21, 2003.

26. Quoted in PBS, "Liberians Storm Port, Rebels Prepare to Leave Capital," August 13, 2003. www.pbs.org.

27. Quoted in Tim Weiner, "Liberia's Split Families Heal, Child by Lost Child," *New York Times,* August 22, 2003.

28. Quoted in Tim Weiner, "At Fourteen, a Liberian War Veteran Dreams of Finding a Way Home," *New York Times,* August 23, 2003.

29. Quoted in Weiner, "At Fourteen."

30. Ezekiel Pajibo, "Liberia: Laying the Foundation for Sustained Peace," *Perspective,* September 16, 2003. www.the perspective.org.

31. Associated Press, "Nigeria Warns Taylor: No Liberia Meddling," *New York Times,* September 16, 2003.

Chronology

1816
The American Colonization Society (ACS), whose purpose is to resettle free persons of color in Africa, is founded in America.

1820
The ACS sends its first group of immigrants to West Africa, landing at Sheba Island in Sierra Leone.

1821
The ACS sends another group of settlers to Africa, picks up the first group from Sierra Leone, and establishes the first official settlement on Cape Mesurado, now part of the capital city of Monrovia.

1822
Jehudi Ashmun, a white Methodist minister and teacher, is appointed by ACS as its agent in Liberia. Ashmun helps to organize the early settlement.

1824
The settlement is named Monrovia after U.S. president James Monroe, and the colony is formally named Liberia.

1838
All of the colonies except the colony called Maryland join together to create the Commonwealth of Liberia and adopt a constitution. Joseph Jenkins Roberts, a trader and successful military commander, is named the first lieutenant governor and becomes the first African American governor of the colony after the governor dies in 1841.

1847
July 26—Liberia officially proclaims its independence.

1848
The first elections are held in the new republic, and Joseph Jenkins Roberts becomes Liberia's first president.

1851
Liberia College is founded.

1857
Maryland becomes a county of Liberia.

1862
The American president, Abraham Lincoln, extends official recognition to Liberia.

1869
The True Whig Party is founded by Americo-Liberians. In the late nineteenth century, it becomes the dominant political party in Liberia.

1885
A treaty is signed ending a border dispute with Britain over Liberia's northern border, and Liberia agrees to give up northern lands to Sierra Leone.

1892
Liberia is forced by France to relinquish its claim to lands in southern Liberia.

1926
Liberia, in exchange for a $5 million loan, permits an American company, Firestone Tire and Rubber Company, to establish a large commercial rubber plantation in the country.

1929
An international commission finds that Liberian officials, including the republic's vice president, profited from indigenous people's forced labor.

1942
Liberia enters World War II on the side of the Allies and allows the United States to construct a major airport and military base in Liberia.

1944
William V.S. Tubman is elected Liberia's president as part of the True Whig Party.

1946
Tubman extends the right to vote and participate in elections to Liberia's indigenous peoples.

1971
After President Tubman's death, William R. Tolbert becomes president.

1979
April 14—a rally protesting the increase of rice prices ends in rioting.

1980
A military coup led by Samuel K. Doe, a Liberian of tribal descent, assassinates President Tolbert and overthrows the government, imposing military rule.

1985
Elections are held and Doe is elected president, restoring civilian rule to Liberia and ending the 133-year rule of the Americo-Liberian True whig Party.

1986
A new constitution is written.

1989
Charles Taylor leads a rebel group to topple the Doe government, leading to Liberia's first civil war.

1990
A West African peacekeeping force is formed to maintain order in Liberia, but rebel forces nevertheless execute Liberia's former head of state, Samuel K. Doe.

1995
The Economic Community of West African States (ECOWAS) brokers a peace treaty between Liberia's warring factions and creates an interim government to plan for elections. The cease-fire is broken by renewed fighting.

1997
Charles Taylor wins the presidency by a wide margin and his National Patriotic Front of Liberia wins overwhelming majorities in the Liberian House and Senate.

1999
Ghana, Nigeria, the United States, and Britain accuse Liberia of fomenting war in neighboring Sierra Leone. Liberians United for Reconciliation and Democracy (LURD), a rebel group that opposes Taylor's government, is founded.

2001

The United Nations imposes sanctions on Liberian diamonds and issues a travel ban on Liberian government officials because of Taylor's support of the rebels in Sierra Leone.

2003

April—A new rebel group, the Movement for Democracy in Liberia (MODEL), begins operations in southeastern Liberia, and both LURD and MODEL make substantial progress in their fight against Taylor's government troops.

June/July—Several attempts are made to negotiate a cease-fire between LURD, MODEL, and the Liberian government, but talks collapse and international pressure mounts for a peacekeeping mission to move into Liberia.

August—Liberian president Charles Taylor agrees, after international pressure, to resign and begin exile in Nigeria. A peace treaty is signed and West African peacekeeping forces, with limited U.S. assistance, move into Monrovia to monitor the cease-fire and prepare the country for elections. Moses Blah, Taylor's vice president, acts as president until an interim government can take over.

October—UN forces take over the peacekeeping function from West African peacekeepers. Charles Gyude Bryant becomes chairman of an interim government that is charged with stabilizing the country and holding elections by 2005.

FOR FURTHER READING

BOOKS

Amy Bronwen, *Beyond the Mango Tree*. New York: Greenwillow Books, 1998. A fictional story about a twelve-year-old Liberian girl and her life.

Jo Mary Sullivan, *Liberia in Pictures*. Minneapolis: Lerner, 1989. An entertaining and readable overview of Liberia geared to young adults.

WEBSITES

BBC News (http://news.bbc.co.uk). This website, run by the British Broadcasting Corporation, provides a short overview and information about Liberia.

PBS (www.pbs.org). A website run by the Public Broadcasting Service provides recent news articles about the 2003 peacekeeping effort in Liberia.

The Perspective (www.theperspective.org). An online publication that contains many articles discussing the problems of Liberia, run by the Liberian Democratic Future (LDF), a group of Liberians from different backgrounds dedicated to pluralistic, democratic Liberia.

U.S. Central Intelligence Agency (CIA) (www.cia.gov). A U.S. government website for the CIA, providing geographical, political, economic, and other information on Liberia.

WORKS CONSULTED

BOOKS

G.E. Gaegbe Boley, *Liberia: The Rise and Fall of the First Republic*. London: Macmillan Education, 1983. A history of Liberia with a focus on the reasons for the 1980 coup written by a member of the Tolbert administration.

C. Abayomi Cassell, *Liberia: History of the First African Republic*. New York: Fountainhead, 1970. A detailed history of Liberia's early history, from its founding in 1847 to 1900, written by a former attorney general of Liberia.

Stephen Ellis, *The Mask of Anarchy*. New York: New York University Press, 1999. A study of civil war in Liberia with a focus on its religious dimensions.

Major I.A. Nass, *A Study in Internal Conflicts: The Liberian Crisis and the West African Peace Initiative*. Nigeria: Fourth Dimension, 2000. A detailed history of the Liberian civil war and crisis of 1989–1997 and the West African peacekeeping effort.

Thomas D. Roberts et al., *Area Handbook for Liberia*. Washington, DC: Foreign Area Studies, American University, 1972. This book provides an overview of Liberia's physical, social, political, and economic institutions and history.

Tom W. Shick, *Behold the Promised Land*. Baltimore, MD: Johns Hopkins University Press, 1980. An exploration of early settler society in nineteenth-century Liberia and its interaction with indigenous cultures.

PERIODICALS

Lawrence K. Altman, "W.H.O., Declaring Crisis, Plans a Big Push with AIDS Drugs," *New York Times*, September 22, 2003.

Associated Press, "Liberia's Taylor Won't Give Up Empire," *New York Times*, September 8, 2003.

————, "Nigeria Warns Taylor: No Liberia Meddling," *New York Times,* September 16, 2003.

Anthony Daniels, "Big Men, Big Corruption: The Way It's Done on the (Not So) Dark Continent," *National Review,* August 11, 2003.

Erik Eckholm, "North Korea Presses Demand for Direct Talks with U.S.," *New York Times,* January 31, 2003.

Hudson Morgan, "Bad Company—Peacekeeping, Nigerian-style," *New Republic,* August 18, 2003.

People Weekly, "Young Guns," August 18, 2003.

Kwaku Sakyi-Addo, "Liberia's Chief Wants Amnesty, Not Trials," *New York Times,* August 22, 2003.

Tim Weiner, "An Army of Educators Saves a Liberian College," *New York Times,* August 26, 2003.

————, "At Fourteen, a Liberian War Veteran Dreams of Finding a Way Home," *New York Times,* August 23, 2003.

————, "Liberia's Split Families Heal, Child by Lost Child," *New York Times,* August 22, 2003.

————, "A Man Without Enemies," *New York Times,* August 21, 2003.

————,"Peacekeepers Take Liberia, Foot by Foot," *New York Times,* August 18, 2003.

INTERNET SOURCES

All About Liberia, May 23, 2003. www.allaboutliberia.com.

BBC News, "Country Profile: Liberia," August 19, 2003. http://news.bbc.co.uk.

Bong Town, "Liberia: The Gem of Africa," 1979. www.bongtown.com.

Terence Burlij, "Liberia's Uneasy Peace: A Profile of Charles Taylor," PBS Online Newshour, 2003. www.pbs.org.

CBC, "Bush Repeats Call for Liberian President to Step Down," July 3, 2003. www.cbc.ca.

Abdoulaye W. Dukule, "Can the New Liberian Transitional Government Suceed?" *The Perspective,* September 16, 2003. www.theperspective.org.

Earth Crash Earth Spirit, "Documenting the Collapse of a Dying Planet," May 20, 2001. http://eces.org.

Encyclopaedia Brittanica. http://search.eb.com.

David Goodman, "Trading on Liberia: Is Firestone Paying for Its Faulty Tires by Shortchanging African Workers?" *Mother Jones,* May/June 2001. www.motherjones.com.

Brent Huffman, "Hexaprotodon Liberiensis: Pygmy Hippopotamus," Ultimate Ungulate, September 8, 2003. www.ultimate ungulate.com.

International Medical Corps, "International Medical Corps Expands Health Care Services to Communities Outside Monrovia," September 8, 2003. www.imcla.com.

Johanna Landeryou, "Hexaprotodon Liberiensis: Pygmy Hippopotamus," The Animal Diversity Web, University of Michigan, November 19, 1997. http://animaldiversity.ummz.umich.edu.

Library of Congress, Federal Research Division, *Liberia: A Country Study,* ed. Harold D. Nelson, 1985. www.global security.org.

MBendi, "Liberia: Overview," February 13, 2001. www.mbendi.co.za.

Phillip M. Mobbs, "The Mineral Industry of Liberia." http://minerals.usgs.gov.

Ezekiel Pajibo, "Liberia: Laying the Foundation for Sustained Peace," *Perspective,* September 16, 2003, www.the perspective.org.

PBS, "Liberians Storm Port, Rebels Prepare to Leave Capital," August 13, 2003. www.pbs.org.

Reuters, "Liberian Timber Industry at Standstill—UN," August 7, 2003. www.alertnet.org.

Mark Scheffler, "Scare Tactics: Why Are Liberian Soldiers Wearing Fright Wigs?" MSN, August 1, 2003. http://slate.msn.com.

Karla Stang, "Saving Liberia's Rainforests," San Diego Earth Times, August 1994. www.sdearthtimes.com.

Tim Sullivan, "Old Ruling Elite Making a Comeback in Liberia," Associated Press, September 29, 2001. www.global security.org.

Joseph K. Tellewoyan, "HIV/AIDS: The Liberian Experience," n.d. http://pages.prodigy.net.

United Nations, "UN Agency Presses for Help as Thousands of Liberian Refugees Remain in Limbo," February 14, 2003. www.un.org.

United Nations Office for the Coordination of Humanitarian Affairs (OCHA), "Liberia: Situation in Monrovia Becoming Desperate," July 21, 2003. www.reliefweb.int.

University of Pennsylvania, School of Arts and Sciences, "Liberia." www.sas.upenn.edu.

U.S. Central Intelligence Agency, "The World Factbook 2003, Liberia." www.cia.org.

U.S. Department of State, Bureau of Democracy, Human Rights, and Labor, "Liberia Country Report on Human Rights Practices for 1998," February 26, 1999. http://pages.prodigy.net.

Vanderkraaij.net, "William V.S. Tubman, President of Liberia (1944–1971)." www.vanderkraaij.net.

Voice of America, "Reduction in West Africa's Rainforests," October 24, 1996. http://forests.org.

World Gazetteer, "Liberia 2003 Cities and Places," 2003. www.world-gazetteer.com.

Yahoo Travel, "Liberia Transportation." http://travel.yahoo.com.

INDEX

PICTURE CREDITS

About the Author

Debra A. Miller is a writer and lawyer with an interest in current events and history. She began her law career in Washington, D.C., where she worked on legislative, policy, and legal matters in government, public interest, and private law firm positions. She has written and edited numerous publications for legal publishers, as well as books and anthologies on historical and political topics. She now lives with her husband in Encinitas, California.